# LEBRON, INC.

# Also by Brian Windhorst

*Return of the King: LeBron James, the Cleveland Cavaliers and the Greatest Comeback in NBA History* (with Dave McMenamin)

# LEBRON, INC.

## The Making of a
## Billion-Dollar Athlete

---

# by Brian Windhorst

**GRAND CENTRAL**
**PUBLISHING**

NEW YORK    BOSTON

Grand Central Publishing
Hachette Book Group
1290 Avenue of the Americas, New York, NY 10104
grandcentralpublishing.com
twitter.com/grandcentralpub

First published in hardcover and ebook in April 2019
First Trade Edition: April 2020

Grand Central Publishing is a division of Hachette Book Group, Inc. The Grand Central Publishing name and logo is a trademark of Hachette Book Group, Inc.

The publisher is not responsible for websites (or their content) that are not owned by the publisher.

The Hachette Speakers Bureau provides a wide range of authors for speaking events. To find out more, go to www.hachettespeakersbureau.com or call (866) 376-6591.

Library of Congress Cataloging-in-Publication Data has been applied for.

ISBNs: 978-1-5387-3085-0 (trade edition), 978-1-5387-3086-7 (ebook)

Printed in the United States of America

LSC-C

10 9 8 7 6 5 4 3 2 1

*For Dane*

# CONTENTS

# LEBRON, INC.

At its core, a professional basketball team isn't all that different from an average high school squad.

There are fights over minutes, shots, and roles. The good times come from camaraderie, teamwork, and winning. Some people love the coach, some people hate the coach. But there is one major difference that separates the NBA from every other league on earth:

The money.

## Chapter 1

# THE POWER OF SAYING NO

Over the years, people have often asked me what the most impressive thing about LeBron James is. It's a challenging question, one I didn't know how to respond to for a long time. Eventually I came to believe in an answer, one that was revealing.

I met LeBron in 1999 when he was fourteen and very much a kid. He had a bit of a baby face and the build of someone who you knew was going to eventually become a big man. He had large feet and long legs, but he didn't need to shave. His teammate at the time and now one of his best friends, Maverick Carter, remembers that LeBron was barely six feet tall when he showed up in the fall of his freshman year at St. Vincent–St. Mary. I remember him being a little taller, but neither of us debate that by the time spring arrived and he was playing in front of a sellout crowd at the state basketball tournament that he was nearing 6-4.

His frame is certainly one of the things many people were stunned by when they first met LeBron, especially before he was on national television every other night. And indeed that is one of the most impressive things about him. He's 6-8 and has carried as much as 280 pounds during his NBA career—these are simply outrageous dimensions for an elite athlete even when surrounded by other elite athletes. The first strength coach LeBron worked with when he was seventeen told me he'd never seen a teenager's body take to weight lifting like LeBron's did, he added muscle so quickly. By the time he entered the NBA he was 240 pounds and didn't just hold his own but was able to dominate the grown men he played against every night.

During a playoff game in 2006, James twisted his ankle and spent more than an hour in the training room getting treatment. There was a real concern that he might miss the next game. I asked Larry Hughes, his Cleveland Cavaliers teammate, if he was worried. "No. Have you seen his ankles?" It was true, LeBron's ankles are the size of an average man's shoulder. Once, when he was in Miami, LeBron *gained* seven pounds during a playoff game. This seems impossible and even LeBron can't explain it, other than to say he ate some protein bars at halftime and drank a lot of water.

There's also LeBron's feel for the game. He's a

wonderful passer, a master of creating angles and delivering to teammates. He's left-handed but plays basketball right-handed, which gives him a measure of ambidexterity that few players can match. This has helped make him a dominating scorer, one of the best ever.

His memory is a vital tool, and it's both short- and long-term. After a game in the 2018 playoffs, James went point by point over a vital two-minute stretch with such rich detail that some in the press conference just started clapping. What they don't know is he can do the same thing for a game from ten years before. "One time we were watching an NFL game on a Sunday," said former Miami Heat teammate Chris Bosh. "So he knows every player. But he knows where every player went to school. Like how is he going to know the backup safety went to Colorado State?"

There's his work ethic, his speed, his durability. All of these are pillars in his case for being one of the greatest basketball players ever. But it isn't what is most impressive about him—to me at least.

To me, it's his awareness.

I've never met anyone who has the awareness of LeBron Raymone James. His awareness of what's happening in the game around him. The way he can see something two or three steps ahead. How he will know just where a teammate will be so he can put the ball there and whether that guy likes to have the seams on the ball vertical or horizontal when it arrives. He can anticipate where an opponent might go or what side of the basket he'll go on.

On perhaps the most important play of his career, when he blocked Andre Iguodala in the final minutes of game 7 of the 2016 Finals, James went up with a hand on either side of the basket. That's because he knew Iguodala liked to attempt reverse layups, and he was defending him going either direction. That's awareness. But that's not the point.

LeBron's awareness of who is in the room, what time and place he's in, and his sense of history are overwhelming. He will sit in the locker room watching a game on television and predict what play will happen next, answer a question from a reporter he knows has flown in to try to trap him into a certain answer, and monitor what two teammates might be talking about in a huddle a few lockers away. That description may seem over the top, but believe me, that's how he can operate.

This awareness has been at the bedrock of James's success off the court as well. His ability to understand what he doesn't know and how to ask for help in these areas has been vital for the expansion of his business empire. His sense of whom he can take advantage of and who are trying to take advantage of him has served him immensely well. It may seem a little coarse, but it's true. LeBron's awareness of how he can use his celebrity and popularity to gain leverage in business transactions has fed his bottom line and enabled him to funnel money to charities he cares about without having to reach into his own pocket.

That is not to say he's been infallible. Like everyone, he's made mistakes. But his ability to have perspective has often softened their blow and helped turn missteps into lessons.

His awareness helped him navigate what he says was one of the most important decisions of his life. It happened on a Thursday night in May 2003 during his senior year of high school. It was in Canton, Massachusetts, in a boardroom with a man holding a $10 million check with his name on it.

So many years later some of the memories of those in the room have gotten a little muddy. LeBron said he watched Paul Fireman, the powerful man who ran Reebok, write the check. His agent at the time said it was already made out, a cashier's check produced from a bank envelope.

What no one forgets is that an eighteen-year-old who had grown up with nothing said no. In fact, he said no to a deal that would have been worth up to $100 million in total and the huge check he could have taken with him and deposited the next morning. A few things went through James's mind when he saw the check. The Reebok executives had done their homework and made sure his mother, Gloria James, was not only in the room when the offer was made but that they handed her the check.

The first thought LeBron had with that eight-figure check in his palm was that his mom's rent at their government-subsidized apartment back in Akron, Ohio, was once seventeen dollars a month. There was a time when the Jameses lived in a housing project in a valley, a place in the city known as "the bottom." LeBron said that when he lived there he was sometimes even afraid of going to the top of the hill. Those who lived at the top of the hill knew to stay clear of the Elizabeth Park housing project because it was a hub of violence. LeBron heard gunshots and saw stabbing victims as a child. He often says he's supposed to be a statistic, that he shouldn't be who he is, that he never should have made it. Elizabeth Park was full of statistics.

Over the top of the housing development was a long, high bridge known in Akron as the Y-Bridge for its shape as it spanned two sections of the city. At one end there was a hospital with a psych ward. For decades the fence that ran the length of the bridge was low and easily scalable. Like Elizabeth Park below, it had a nickname too: the suicide bridge. Sometimes, kids playing at their rusty playground below it saw bodies falling.

The second thing LeBron thought about, though, was the other offers. This was his first shoe meeting. He'd declared he was going pro a few weeks earlier. Reebok had the leadoff spot. They'd sent a private jet to come pick him up after school that day. There was a trip to Los Angeles set up the next day for him to hear Adidas's pitch. The next week another trip was planned to Portland to visit Nike.

Reebok wanted LeBron to cancel those trips. They wanted him to sign with them in that moment. In an attempted shock and awe moment, they made one of the most extraordinary endorsement contract offers that's ever been made to a basketball player.

The idea came from Steve Stoute, a former music industry executive who launched the careers of dozens of artists from Will Smith to 50 Cent to Nas. Stoute was working for Reebok and urged Fireman to do what he'd done with many talented teenagers who had come from poverty. Show them the money, and it closes the deal. A few months before, Stoute had helped Reebok close a deal with Jay-Z, and his first signature shoe, the S. Carter, had just launched.

"This happened all the time in the music business: Give the guy a big advance and they do the deal," Stoute said. "This wasn't short money. We were offering him the deal he wanted. He liked what we had to say, and he took the meeting, so we knew we were an option. We assumed if we gave him his price that he'd take it."

The Reebok executives left the room to let LeBron think about it with one caveat: It was an exploding offer. Take the deal then and he could have the bonus check, but if he walked away the bonus would, too. Some could say that LeBron saying no was brilliant. Some could say it was too risky. He had an experienced agent, Aaron Goodwin, with him and was getting advice, but no one would have blamed him for saying yes. Even Nike and Adidas would have understood him saying yes. It was the type of offer you probably shouldn't say no to.

At eighteen, even with his whole life basically in front of him, LeBron had the awareness to say no.

"I clapped in the room," Stoute said. "Fireman couldn't believe it; it made no sense to him. I knew I'd seen something I'd never seen before. I clapped out of respect. I'd been around young, professional, and successful African Americans that had come from meager circumstances for years. And when LeBron said no to that money in that room, I realized that we as a generation had evolved. I was blown away. He turned the money down and went to homeroom the next day!"

"You have to think of the back end," LeBron told me a few years later. "I was going to be making a deal for life. You don't think about the first check; you think about all of them."

Having that type of awareness is the basis for this story. This book will chronicle LeBron's journey off the floor, which has run parallel to his unique playing career. As with the game, he's had incredible victories and humbling defeats. Fallout from some choices has been just as bitter as losses in the Finals. Some victories have brought him enormous satisfaction, even if it stayed largely private. This book will detail both.

In a way, this is only the start of LeBron's business career: He's planning for the forty or so years after his basketball career ends. LeBron and his family, friends, and business partners have grand plans that could make what's happened so far just an introduction. LeBron set his sights on becoming a billionaire long ago and has evolved into not just counting money but expanding influence through ownership. Ownership of brick-and-mortar businesses. Ownership of intellectual property. Even ownership of professional sports franchises.

How he's gotten this far, though, is a remarkable story. And you're about to read it.

# Chapter 2

# THE BAG MAN

**A**s she finished a cigarette outside a small college gym in Hackensack, New Jersey, Gloria James laughed when I asked her about Las Vegas. It was the first week of July 2001 at a showcase event for young basketball players, the Adidas ABCD Camp, and her son was having one of the most important weeks of his teenage years.

LeBron was headed to Vegas the following week for a tournament, and Gloria told me she was planning to go. We were just killing time out in the sun between games. The gym was packed and hot. I made small talk about slot machines. "Brian, I don't have two nickels to rub together," she said. "I'm not putting anything in those machines."

The summer of 2001 was a momentous time to be a high school basketball star. That June the NBA fully fell in love with high school prospects. It had been building for a few years, starting with Kevin Garnett leaping from high school in 1995 and then Kobe Bryant the following year. Both had become stars, and the league was looking for more. In 2001, four of the top eight players taken were straight from high school, including the first-ever number one overall pick, Kwame Brown. As a result, the pro scouts were swarming the ABCD Camp and getting side-eyed in the process from the top college coaches who had a new level of competition now.

A few months earlier Matt Doherty, then the coach at North Carolina, was trying to talk a high-profile commitment named DeSagana Diop out of going straight to the NBA from high school. He drove to a meeting with Diop at Oak Hill Academy in Virginia and showed him a list of the salaries for first-round picks. Doherty was trying to show Diop if he came and played for the Tar Heels for a year and made himself into a top pick he'd earn a lot more than if he entered the draft that year and was taken late in the first round, where he was projected.

It was a reasonable pitch. The previous fall, I'd also made the drive to Mouth of Wilson, Virginia, to Oak Hill and spoke with Diop. He wasn't sure he was ready for the league. But when Diop looked at Doherty's printout he saw that even the last picks of the first round were guaranteed a three-year contract at nearly a million per year. Diop, who was from Senegal and never dreamed of such wealth, decided to enter the draft practically on the spot. (He ended up getting picked eighth and made $1.8 million his first season.)

As such, the college coaches and pro scouts were elbow-to-elbow at the ABCD. It was a bizarre time, as the pro scouts were allowed to watch the kids but not, per NBA rules, talk to them; while the college coaches were allowed to talk to them but not, per NCAA rules, mention their names to the media. LeBron, who was just sixteen and still growing, was the consensus best player at the event as he put on a show for three straight days and soundly outperformed some of the older players at the camp. Rick Pitino, who had just been hired to coach at Louisville, emerged from the gym that afternoon and told television cameras that LeBron—without using his name, one of the NCAA rules Pitino apparently followed (he lost his job years later after the school was accused of violations)—was headed for NBA stardom.

Ira Berkow, a Pulitzer Prize–winning columnist from the *New York Times*, came across the Hudson River and watched LeBron for an afternoon during the camp. In the *Times* the next day, Berkow proclaimed that he could probably go pro after his upcoming junior year of high school. It was the brightest national media spotlight that'd been shined on LeBron to that point, and it created a little bit of a frenzy. Sonny Vaccaro, the amateur basketball legend who famously recruited Michael

Jordan to Nike and Kobe Bryant to Adidas during his long and prolific career, told me LeBron might have been a lottery pick in the high school–laden draft that'd just taken place because he was already better than all the eighteen-year-olds who had been picked.

Naturally Vaccaro was going to be complimentary. He was in full-out recruit mode by that point, having arranged for LeBron's high school team to get a contract with Adidas that would outfit him in gear from head to toe. LeBron's freshman year, he couldn't wear his preferred number 23 because the school only had even-numbered jerseys, and new uniforms were purchased once every few years. By the time he was a senior, LeBron had worn more than a dozen varieties of uniform designs, and he wore a new pair of Adidas shoes nearly every game. Bottom line, though, Vaccaro was right: He was better than all of them.

While they had a pretty good idea he was headed to the NBA in the near future, the reality of the situation hit LeBron and his family that week. Not only was it clear that he wasn't ever going to college, but he was going to be the target of shoe companies who were always interested in capturing a star to help market their product. The reason is pretty basic: The earlier a shoe company could identify a possible star, the better they can develop a relationship and try to box out competitors and sign him to a more reasonable deal. As the Reebok executive Steve Stoute said, young basketball players are comparable to young music artists in this way. An important difference, though, is that a record label can find and sign young talent immediately, no matter their age, to make sure competitors couldn't get a chance. Because of the amateurism rules that govern high school sports, shoe companies have to wait. That only makes the stakes and the competition higher and hotter.

This set of circumstances swings both ways: There's a measure of pressure on the young athletes to increase demand and to perform under pressure. Yes, it was clear LeBron was one of the select few who had a legitimate chance to make it big in the world of basketball. But he'd also have to maintain the momentum. If he could have signed a multimillion-dollar deal at age sixteen, he would have. But he couldn't play in the NBA for two years, and a lot of things could change in that span. To make sure LeBron got the best coaching, competition, and exposure, he was going to need to travel the country more than ever before. And Gloria, who had struggled her entire life, clearly didn't have the resources to make this possible.

That's what struck me as Gloria made the offhand comment about the slot machines. First off, she'd already hit the lottery. Her son was going to be in position to make massive sums of money. But there was a lot of spending already going on. LeBron always just showed up places, had new stuff, was well fed, and had a car to get around and a place to stay. The money had to come from somewhere, and it wasn't coming from his mom. And there was going to be a lot more of that in the next couple of years.

What was happening was one of the first lessons LeBron would learn about the business world.

Eddie Jackson had known Gloria and LeBron for years. When LeBron was young, Eddie and Gloria were a couple. There's a well-known photo of LeBron playing with a miniature basketball hoop he got for Christmas as a young child. Jackson claims to have been the one who bought it for him. Gloria and Eddie's relationship was over by the time LeBron was in high school, but he was still providing for the family in some ways.

At the time, Jackson described himself simply as "a businessman." He did have some legitimate dealings as a promoter, but by his own admission, he was a criminal. He spent time in jail on drug charges when LeBron was younger. But while LeBron was in high school, Jackson was running a real estate fraud scheme that ended up getting him sent to federal prison after a plea bargain when LeBron was a senior.

These facts led many to assume that Jackson had nefarious intentions, and they saw his connection to LeBron as a character flaw in both men. Clearly, it was not ideal for LeBron and his family to be involved with, and perhaps benefiting from, a felon. But the truth is that Jackson's role was more nuanced and, at times, rather important. He was the one who helped get LeBron his first car. Eventually he allowed LeBron to move into a house he owned. He bankrolled some of the trips LeBron took and made sure Gloria got there too, so that LeBron was more comfortable. Jackson was the closest thing LeBron had to a father and, for a time, LeBron even called him his father. Did Jackson do this with money he earned through fraud? Maybe. Did he have some side deals working where he benefited from James and probably saw some of the endeavor as a long-term way to enrich himself? Perhaps. But it doesn't mean he wasn't important to LeBron's journey. And it doesn't mean that Jackson didn't care for LeBron and try to protect him, which he absolutely did.

When Jackson saw the situation developing around LeBron in 2001, he knew he needed help funding what was becoming quite the operation. Through a mutual friend, he arranged a meeting with a man named Joe Marsh, who at the time was one of the richest people in LeBron's hometown of Akron, Ohio. Marsh had largely earned his fortune as an agent and promoter himself, just on a massive and much more legitimate scale. His specialty was setting up tours for big-name acts. His clients included David Copperfield, Janet Jackson, Fleetwood Mac, and others. If you ever went to a Lord of the Dance show, chances are it was a Marsh production. A few years earlier he and his partner had sold their company for $118 million, making him fabulously wealthy.

Jackson saw Marsh as a solution to a problem. Marsh's intentions seemed to be all business: He wanted to create a connection to what he, correctly, saw as a potential cash cow. Jackson and Marsh agreed to a transaction. Shortly after James returned from New Jersey with the belief that he was headed toward being a number one draft pick, Marsh gave Jackson a $30,000 check. It was the first installment of what ended up being a $100,000 loan to Eddie and Gloria over the next two years. It was hardly a favor. Marsh had Jackson sign a document that put a 10 percent annual interest rate on the loan and guaranteed the full rights to a documentary LeBron was expected to take part in. Plus there was an agreement to participate in endorsement deals for LeBron in the future.

Marsh obviously was a successful businessman. This could have been seen as a shrewd move, not unlike an angel investor getting in early to fund a startup and then being in a position to amplify his investment first when the stock took off. Others might say it was usury disguised as a helping hand, a veteran of the entertainment business taking advantage of some naivete. What it is fair to say is that Marsh was dealing with an in-over-her-head Gloria and a young and inexperienced LeBron, who barely seemed to know what was going on when he was brought to a meeting at Marsh's mansion on a lake outside Akron after the deal was finalized.

From some people's viewpoint, LeBron and his family

taking part in a cash-for-influence deal from an agent like this spoiled his amateur status on the spot. Had this come to light at that time, he probably would have been banned from playing high school sports and been shamed in the process. But considering the landscape, which side was acting in poor faith gets a little more complex.

Only Jackson knows how much of that loan he actually spent on the family. Maybe he spent it all on them. By the time the payments ended, Jackson was in prison and Marsh was sending monthly checks directly to Gloria. Though LeBron met Marsh, he never signed anything, and that ended up becoming important. Over the next eighteen months, LeBron had a couple of meetings about the documentary and showed some interest in taking part. But LeBron's interest waned after his high school team was upset in the state championship game his junior year, triggering a wave of criticism that started to sour LeBron on the media for the first time. Also, LeBron was getting more famous.

He'd been on the cover of *Sports Illustrated*. He met Michael Jordan. He had less interest in working on a film with someone he'd never heard of. After meeting Spike Lee at an event when he was seventeen, James told Marsh he wanted to have Lee direct the documentary. Marsh tried to accommodate him but had trouble even reaching Lee. The documentary never got off the ground, and LeBron and Gloria ending up cutting off communication with Marsh. By the time LeBron was a high school senior, access to money and credit was no longer an issue. It was harsh, but to them, Marsh had served his purpose.

Frustrated he'd been cut out, Marsh sued James during the first month of his rookie season for $15 million for money lost on the documentary and possible marketing deals. He said LeBron had breached oral contracts, even though those oral contracts were arranged when he was a juvenile. Marsh said he didn't want to be LeBron's agent and barely knew who he was when the loan was made; he was just making a business transaction, and his business partner had not lived up to their end of the deal.

Though LeBron tried to settle and offered to repay the loan through his agent and attorneys over the course of months, the case eventually went to trial in 2005 and he had to testify. By then, LeBron was so closely watched that his order for lunch in the courthouse cafeteria (two chicken sandwiches and cupcakes for dessert) and method of payment (a $100 bill) were reported in the local paper. By a vote of 6–2, the jury sided with James, and he ended up simply repaying the loan with interest.

He was just twenty years old when he sat on the stand, four years removed from when the loan was arranged around him. He toyed with the opposing attorney's questions, played to the crowd in the courtroom, and ended up with a win. Coming from a family that "didn't have two nickels to rub together," LeBron wrote the check for $122,000 on the spot and moved on with his head held high.

When he was sixteen and this untidy arrangement was conceived, LeBron was beginning to understand he was going to be a professional basketball player. By the time this ruling came, he'd become acquainted with the power and leverage he could wield. The difference was unmistakable as was the fact that LeBron had full control of his affairs by then.

The LeBron who sat quietly on a couch when the adults around him made a six-figure deal became an all-encompassing force that controlled the courtroom because of his maturity, to be sure. But it also was because of the invaluable lessons he learned when putting together his shoe deal, which stands as one of the most important moments in his life.

# Chapter 3

# THE DEAL OF A LIFETIME

In 1971, Phil Knight was running a fledgling shoe distribution company, working from a small office outside Portland, Oregon. He was struggling to come up with a name for a new brand he was developing, one whose tread design had been inspired by a waffle iron. He wanted to call the new line Dimension Six. Knight had an MBA and was a CPA and a fearless entrepreneur, but he was not a specialist in marketing. His employees begged him not to go with that name. He fought them. After days of going back and forth, he was exasperated. With the factory needing an answer, he went with an employee's last-ditch idea: Nike, the Greek god of victory.

At the time, Nike was doing about $1 million in annual sales and sometimes struggling to make payroll. By 2003, Nike had become one of the world's dominant brands, taking in more than $10 billion in revenue. Along his remarkable journey, Knight learned many lessons. One of the most important was the value of marketing. It had superior shoes for decades, but Nike didn't become an international juggernaut until it became a superior marketer. Perhaps no one meant more to Nike in this effort than Michael Jordan, who signed with the firm in 1984. A year later, when the first Air Jordans were released, they sold more than $70 million worth of product in just the first two months. Recruiting and landing top basketball players as endorsers has been vital to Nike ever since.

In early 2003 there was a brewing battle among the big three shoe companies over five major basketball stars who were coming on the market. Kobe Bryant, who had been with Adidas since he entered the NBA in 1996, had gotten out of the contract so he could become a shoe free agent. Another prospect was Yao Ming, the gateway to hundreds of millions of Chinese basketball fans, who had been signed with Nike when he entered the NBA the year before. Star Kevin Garnett had been with And 1, a relatively obscure company, and was also a free agent. Then there were the two rookies-to-be who had generated major buzz: LeBron James and Carmelo Anthony. LeBron was the highest-profile high school player in history, and Anthony had become a star in his one season at Syracuse, leading the team to the national championship.

Over the winter, Knight had told some of his executives that he coveted all of them. He wanted all five in Nikes by the next basketball season. Nike was the global leader in athletic shoe sales and was dominant in basketball by this point. But at the time Adidas was a nearly $7 billion company and Reebok was at more than $3 billion; it was a strong competitive marketplace. Nike may have had the most money, but the goal of landing all five big names meant they'd be somewhat limited in their offers—they couldn't pay all of them top dollar.

In early January 2003, LeBron's high school team flew to Los Angeles to play in a showcase event at UCLA's Pauley Pavilion. The game, against Orange County power Mater Dei, was broadcast on ESPN2 and was the second LeBron game that had been on national TV in a month. It was personal for LeBron and his fellow seniors at St. Vincent–St. Mary. In the summer before their freshman year of high school, that group— LeBron, Dru Joyce, Sian Cotton, and Willie McGee— reached the AAU national championship game in Orlando. They lost a heartbreaker to a team from Southern California, several of whom had gone on to play at Mater Dei. This was a high-stakes get-even game, a showdown of sorts. Plus LeBron and his teammates knew that if they won, they'd ascend to the number one ranking in the various national polls, which was important to them. But there was something else happening that night. It was a Nike-Adidas showdown, too.

Sitting in a baseline seat at one end was Phil Knight himself. It was almost unheard of for the head of Nike to attend a high school game, especially in a recruiting contest. He sat with Lynn Merritt, the Nike executive who had been put in charge of getting LeBron to sign with the company.

Sitting on the other end of the floor was Sonny Vaccaro, the Adidas executive who had made it his mission not just to sign LeBron but to make sure Nike, his former employer and archrival, didn't. Much has been written and said about Vaccaro over the years, more than could possibly be covered in this volume. He found players for colleges and shoe companies; he ended up working for Nike, Adidas, and Reebok before he retired. He paid college coaches to outfit their teams in whatever brand he was selling. And everyone— the players, the coaches, the companies, and Sonny himself—made good money in the process. At least he was generally honest about his role.

In this phase of his career, Vaccaro would routinely play up being the underdog, praise Nike in interviews, and make it seem like he didn't have a fair chance representing little old Adidas. He'd left Nike unpleasantly in 1991. He'd gotten credit for helping them sign Jordan, though three decades later the parties still quarrel over who was truly responsible for landing the company-altering pitchman. Wherever the truth lies, more than a decade after leaving Nike Vaccaro had scored some wins against his old shop. He'd met and bonded with Bryant and landed him for Adidas before Nike could get to him. Then he helped force Bryant to the Los Angeles Lakers with some behind-the-scenes maneuvers that set up the German brand with the perfect marketing machine. That deal paid Bryant a base of $1.5 million a year, a bargain indeed.

The next year, Vaccaro found another high school–to–NBA star he identified through his summer camp, Tracy McGrady, and got him to Adidas before Nike really had a chance. McGrady met with Nike and an offer was made, but he was loyal to Vaccaro, and with a $2 million per year base from Adidas, it was just a formality. By 2003, Bryant and McGrady were driving Adidas's basketball business. Nike had a stable of stars, including high-flyer Vince Carter, but they hadn't done as well getting the straight–from–high-school players that Vaccaro had been beating them to.

Vaccaro was first with LeBron, too, thanks to an arranged meeting in the spring of 2001. Vaccaro had seen some tape on LeBron, but he wasn't blown away. After LeBron's freshman season, Adidas made a deal to supply his high school team with shoes and clothes. The total outlay was $15,000. Vaccaro would later call this one of the best deals he'd ever made. All the way through high school, LeBron had Adidas on his feet for games. He started wearing other models when he was a senior, but he essentially was Team Adidas. In truth, at the start Vaccaro and Adidas were hardly that invested; LeBron was just someone on their radar. There weren't many teenagers from Ohio that got Vaccaro's attention.

But as part of the efforts to broaden his basketball horizons, LeBron had gotten hooked up with the Oakland Soldiers from Northern California for a few tournaments after his sophomore year. The Soldiers had a good reputation, and this was an example of how LeBron was such an outlier. In those days it wasn't unusual for a player to join an AAU team that wasn't close to home, but it was unheard of for a player from Ohio to play with a team based in California.

LeBron had impressed when playing with the Soldiers, too. Two of his teammates were future NBA draft picks—Leon Powe and Kendrick Perkins—and LeBron was still the best player. Both would later be teammates with LeBron in the NBA. When Powe played for the Cavs, he told me he had been surprised how good the kid from Ohio was and then let down when he asked one of his coaches what class LeBron was in. Powe, then the highest-rated player in his class in the nation by some of the recruiting magazines, found out LeBron was his age. He knew he was eventually going to lose his top ranking to LeBron.

Playing in some events out west, LeBron had been seen by some people that Vaccaro trusted, and they told Vaccaro that he should make the effort to get to know the young kid from Akron. With this in mind, a special one-day event was arranged at the University of San Francisco essentially for Vaccaro to see James. Adidas paid for the trip—whoops, another amateurism violation—and LeBron, his teammate Dru Joyce, his mother, and his high school coach, Keith Dambrot, came out to San Francisco.

LeBron was outfitted with Adidas gear for the day, including a pair of shoes with his initials and number 23 on them. That wasn't normal, either. One of Adidas's grassroots recruiters, Chris Rivers, was all in on LeBron and now was trying to convince his boss, Vaccaro, to be as well. One problem was that LeBron wasn't exactly all in on the event. He was just sixteen and not always focused. He was in the middle of a growth spurt, now at 6-6 and over two hundred pounds; his face had broken out, and he'd grown out his hair a little wild. He was getting used to being catered to and fussed over. He could be a bit, well, moody. And he wasn't in the mood. On this day, he didn't like the shorts Adidas had provided him to play in.

In the first game he was messing with them, pulling out his uniform top and retucking it and retying the shorts. Vaccaro had flown up from Los Angeles for this? He was interested in LeBron but not sold. This performance wasn't exactly getting it done. After the first game, Dambrot pulled LeBron out into the hallway. It's a bright space that overlooks a beautiful part of San

Francisco, where on a clear day there are views down the hills to the bay. On the wall is a plaque honoring William Felton Russell, one of the greatest players to ever play. Bill Russell led the USF Dons to two national championships and starred in that building, the War Memorial Gymnasium.

Dambrot wasn't giving history lessons. He frequently yelled. A short man with a slight build and tight, curly hair, Dambrot has a pleasant smile and a disarming personality off the floor. But when he's coaching, he takes on a different demeanor. He was always angry during games, stomping his loafers against the hardwood at mistakes, a constant steely glare on his face. When LeBron came to play for Dambrot in high school, he couldn't believe how much he yelled. It upset LeBron. No, it was more than that. It pissed him off. He hated it. He'd never been yelled at like that by a coach.

Dambrot was delivering another stern message that afternoon. He told him he was blowing this chance. He told him he wasn't focused. He told him there was a lot of money on the line, something a sixteen-year-old doesn't hear too often when playing in what amounted to a glorified pickup game, even if it was absolutely true in this case. And Dambrot told him to stop messing around with his shorts.

LeBron listened. In the second game, LeBron showed his potential. He wowed Vaccaro, especially with a 70-foot pass he threw to a teammate that led to a basket. Vaccaro would talk about seeing that pass for years. Who knows how long it really was; it seems to have grown in the legend. Vaccaro loved the way Le-Bron played, how he looked to get teammates—some of whom he barely knew in this case—involved despite it being an environment that was set up for Vaccaro to see him. A few months later, Vaccaro made sure Le-Bron was the centerpiece attraction at his ABCD Camp in New Jersey, the time when his new protégé would go national.

Fast-forward to that night at UCLA and Vaccaro was sitting with sidekick Chris Rivers, who had become the tip of the spear for Adidas in the fast-developing "get LeBron" mission. He'd moved to Akron for LeBron's senior year so he would always be around and deepen relationships. They stared down at Knight and Merritt on the other side, knowing they had an edge. They knew LeBron, they knew his mom, they knew Eddie Jackson, the surrogate father. They'd been to meals. And, Vaccaro believed, they'd convinced his bosses back in Germany to offer their richest contract ever to make sure they got him.

But Merritt was working, too. He'd been with Nike for more than a decade himself and, like Vaccaro, had become a powerful man just below the surface in the basketball world. He brought Ken Griffey Jr. to Nike and was his mentor at the company. He took care of Scottie Pippen. He recruited and advanced many more stars along the way. And while Vaccaro was working his usual avenues to become connected with James, Merritt made a different play.

Maverick Carter met LeBron when they were still little boys. Carter has said they met when LeBron came to his seventh birthday party. Or maybe it was his eighth. Their parents sort of ran in the same circles, which, to be honest, in part involved drugs. Carter's father, Otis, had had several trips to prison on drug-related charges. Gloria James had had a handful of arrests, mostly for minor offenses.

Carter is a product of this world, which he doesn't shy away from. His grandmother, who was a major force in his early life, ran an all-night gambling club out of her home. Carter hung out there, and sweeping up and running errands for his grandmother was his first job. He describes his dad as a "hustler" but does so with endearment. He always respected what Otis had to do to put food on the table. He was around a lot of older men like that at his grandmother's place.

When Carter was a teenager, he starting selling pot. His mother, Katherine, found his stash in his jacket and hit the ceiling. She had graduated from the University of Akron, working her way through by going to night school, and put in several decades as a social worker for the city of Akron. A hard worker and intelligent woman, she demanded that Carter straighten out his life or he'd end up like his father, in jail.

This and other measures worked; by the time he was a senior in high school at St. Vincent–St. Mary, Carter was a football and basketball star and had landed a full ride scholarship to play basketball at Western Michigan University. He was the captain of the high school team when LeBron was a freshman and was a consummate leader and calming influence. Having seen him play in high school, I'd contend that Carter was a better wide receiver than power forward, though his talents for managing people seemed to be more valuable on the basketball floor. In that way he was like his father: He had a way of dealing with difficult situations. And while his mother didn't always think Otis was a positive influence, there is no doubt some of the lessons he gave Carter contributed to the man he became.

During the one season LeBron and Carter played together there was a vital moment that spoke to the futures of both. It was in the state quarterfinals, known in Ohio as the regional final. The game was at the Canton Memorial Fieldhouse, an old barn next to the Pro Football Hall of Fame. The opponent was a basketball powerhouse school from Cleveland, Villa Angela–St. Joseph, which had produced many stars, including Clark Kellogg, regarded as one of the greatest players in Ohio history.

Early in the fourth quarter of a tight game, Carter fouled out. The game was now on LeBron's shoulders. Carter pulled him aside and told him he could carry the team home. It seems absurd now to think there was doubt, but then LeBron was only fifteen and he had periods where he would become a wallflower. It was one of the habits Dambrot had been trying to drive out of him, sometimes with fiery halftime speeches. Whatever Carter said worked: LeBron was a playmaking whiz over the game's last seven minutes, and his team won.

Carter went on to college, planning to have a career in basketball as a player. But the coach who recruited Carter had been fired, and he didn't play much, averaging just two points a game. The team went 7–21. More sobering, when Carter went to play games at Michigan and then at Indiana that season, he saw he was outclassed by the competition. It turned out that he didn't have a future playing basketball. This is reality for most college players, but it's a credit to Carter that he recognized it so early. After the disappointing freshman year, he transferred to the University of Akron, where Dambrot had become an assistant coach and had a spot for him on the roster.

He had to sit out for a season because of the NCAA's transfer rules. But the side benefit was that he was home, which allowed him to reintegrate back into the day-to-day goings-on with LeBron. This was 2001, that fateful year when James had become a national name and everyone around him started preparations for his pro career. It was also when the shoe company executives started coming around Akron, beginning the recruiting process. Merritt was one of them. As he sat in the stands at games and then hung around afterward to get to know LeBron's friends and family, Merritt quickly identified not only the role that Carter played in LeBron's life but how he thought about the game and about LeBron's future. Merritt then did something that ended up being extremely important: He offered Carter an internship at Nike's headquarters in Beaverton, Oregon.

Merritt was taken with Carter and liked him. But to be clear, the main motive was to establish a connection to LeBron. It's hardly unique: Ever since Nike has had endorsement deals with athletes, they've employed people who are close to them or connected to them. In the 1970s, when Knight badly wanted to get Nikes on track star Steve Prefontaine's feet, he assigned an employee to be a "Pre whisperer." That said, some Nike executives were surprised to see Carter in Beaverton. Typically, Nike picked interns from places like Harvard Business School and Stanford, where Knight had gone to grad school, not the University of Akron.

Carter was ambitious and smart. During assignments at his internship he'd often seek time with bosses and be inquisitive about Nike's processes and motivations. Some at Nike went into working with Carter thinking he was just someone they'd have to put up with as they chased the much bigger prize—this was a stigma that Carter would spend much of the next fifteen years fighting—but he started to show he was more than that. At some point, Carter had come across a quote from Albert Einstein that spoke to him: "I have no special talent. I am only passionately curious." This became a guiding principle of sorts for Carter or, at the very least, a cool thing to say to people to disarm them. Either way, he started saying it a lot and generally following through.

When he got the internship, Carter decided he would quit basketball and quit school in order to prepare to work with LeBron when he became a pro. Carter and LeBron decided Carter would go to work for whichever shoe company LeBron chose to sign with. Carter would be LeBron's man inside. When it has suited him, LeBron has sometimes pled ignorance when it comes to how he viewed the business world when he was in high school. He was inexperienced but never ignorant. His assumption that he could get Carter placed showed that by the time he was seventeen, he had a good grip on the power he was going to wield in this process.

Nike had another ally, and it was a powerful one. When LeBron was sixteen, he and Carter went to Chicago to play in some pickup games with some NBA players. It was getting around just how good this kid from Ohio was, and it was opening some doors. The workouts were at Hoops Gym outside the city, a facility run by well-known trainer Tim Grover. One day Grover asked LeBron to stick around after the workouts ended. Then a high-end sports car pulled into the lot and Michael Jordan got out. LeBron and Carter were numb. Jordan was having some semi-secret workouts as he plotted his final return to the NBA. He spent twenty to thirty minutes getting to know LeBron that day. Of course, Jordan was LeBron's idol, and the moment overwhelmed him. So did Jordan handing over his cell phone number. Over the next few years, when Jordan would come to Cleveland to play with the Washington Wizards, he'd check in with LeBron. In the spring of his senior year, Jordan invited LeBron to play in his annual high school all-star game in Washington, DC, where they spent more time together. Getting to know Jordan, perhaps the signature Nike athlete of all time, added to the allure.

It was true that Vaccaro was there first, had a good relationship with LeBron, and had him in Adidas shoes and in Adidas clothes. But Merritt and Nike had made inroads, too. LeBron knew enough not to lean too much in either direction. The summer before his senior year he attended both Vaccaro's ABCD Camp in New Jersey and the competing Nike All-American Camp in the same week in July. He couldn't play because he'd suffered a broken wrist at a tournament in Chicago in the spring and was still recovering. LeBron held press conferences at both events. When he was at the Adidas camp he wore Nike shoes. When he was at the Nike camp he wore Adidas shoes. The game was on.

That night in Los Angeles in January LeBron didn't play great by his standards: He missed all eight of his three-point attempts and 15 shots in all. After he'd wowed the national television audience a month before in a victory over Oak Hill Academy in Cleveland, this effort was somewhat more muted. But he still scored 21 points with nine rebounds and seven assists. He had several highlight plays, notably a between-the-legs pass that would become a staple on *SportsCenter*. There were 12,000 people there to see it, the biggest crowd at Pauley that season, which was a down year for the Bruins. His team won by six and was indeed ranked number one by *USA Today* the following week. The real high-stakes game came later.

When it came time to get serious, Reebok was behind Nike and Adidas. They hadn't done the same groundwork or invested in creating the relationships. What they had was a tangential connection in William "Wes" Wesley, who was a close friend of Philadelphia 76ers' star Allen Iverson. At the time, Iverson was the face of Reebok basketball. Wesley became better known to the public when he helped break up the brawl in Detroit between the Detroit Pistons and Indiana Pacers in 2004, pulling Ron Artest off the floor as Wesley's suit was doused with beer by irate fans. But Wesley had been an operator in the basketball world long before that. It has been said by agents and league executives that for a time in the mid-2000s he was one of the most influential people in basketball.

Wesley specialized in befriending young players and helping them and their families, an overarching way of saying he was a connector in dealmaking. He called the players his "nephews," and some of them referred to Wesley as "uncle." Many stories about him floated around: that he bailed players out from gambling debts, that he arranged mortgages, that he would fly in on private planes to mediate disputes between star players and coaches. No matter how his role was defined, NBA players trusted him, and college and pro coaches saw him as someone to be respected. There was no doubt Wesley excelled in relationship building. Nike had helped make sure Jordan took an interest in LeBron. Wesley helped arrange another introduction to one of LeBron's heroes, hip-hop mogul Jay-Z.

One of the players Wesley was closest to was Dajuan Wagner. He was more than a nephew: Wagner was Wesley's godson. He also happened to be a rookie with the Cleveland Cavaliers during LeBron's senior year of high school. Wesley and Wagner's father, Milt, had known each other since high school, and Wesley essentially began his career as a basketball power broker as Milt rose up the ranks to the NBA. Wesley later helped Leon Rose, a lawyer from the Philadelphia area, launch his agent business and played a significant role in Rose becoming one of the NBA's most powerful agents. Rose represented Wagner as well. The upshot of all this is that in the 2002–03 season, Wesley was spending a lot of time in Cleveland to support his godson.

Meanwhile, that season James was spending occasional off nights going to Cleveland to watch Cavs games, where he was warmly welcomed and even given locker room access. The Cavs were purposely terrible that season; they were tanking to try to improve their odds of drafting LeBron, and here was LeBron sometimes showing up in the locker room with his high school letterman jacket. And the truth was, he was arguably already the best player in that room. Cavs coach John Lucas had allowed LeBron to work out at the arena while he was a junior in high school, and when the NBA found out they suspended him for two games and fined the team $150,000 because it violated draft rules. But LeBron was around.

This helped Wesley get to know him as well as his friends and family and start a relationship. Just how Wesley got paid and who he was working with at any one time was opaque. But he routinely tried to recruit players to Rose's agency. Rose represented Iverson and negotiated a lifetime deal with Reebok in 2001. When Reebok's private jet touched down in Akron to get LeBron for that pivotal pitch, Wesley was on it as part of the recruitment team.

But there was a reason Reebok was selected to make

the first presentation: They had the most ground to make up. Earlier in the year, Reebok had made Kobe Bryant a huge offer reportedly worth up to $15 million per season. Bryant had paid $8 million to buy himself out of his Adidas deal some months before. As a three-time champion already, Kobe was a major shoe free agent himself and spent the season wearing different brands. But Bryant's talks with Reebok broke down and he ended up focusing on Nike. Aaron Goodwin, who won the agent race to land LeBron as a client in part because he had a history of doing big shoe deals, knew Reebok had struck out with Bryant and designed a strategy to create a bidding war. He hoped Reebok, which was clearly eager to get another star after missing out on Bryant, would set the market. Goodwin had made it clear in speaking with Reebok officials that LeBron expected a huge offer for them to be taken seriously.

Naturally after Reebok made such a compelling move, LeBron reached out to both Merritt and Vaccaro to gauge whether they'd be willing to come up with the same type of offer. There had been a long buildup to this, and everyone had tried to predict how it would go. The money now being discussed was higher than the parties could have dreamed. For the first time, LeBron was starting to realize he might have a future that didn't include Nike or Adidas, the brands in which he'd been envisioning himself for years.

Vaccaro had hinted to LeBron that Adidas was going

to offer $100 million guaranteed, ten years at $10 million per year. A magical and a stunning number, even years later it stands as a benchmark that is hard to fathom. But the scenario of three companies all in the bidding for an asset that each badly wanted had created a situation in which LeBron was going to be able to leverage a historic deal. Vaccaro wanted to win; this one would go down on an already deep résumé.

For his part, Vaccaro had been preparing for this move for months and had spoken to the highest levels of the company to make sure everything was set for his pitch. Significant money had been invested in the weekend meeting. Adidas sent a private jet for LeBron and several of his friends on a Friday, just two days after he'd returned from Reebok. After the party landed, they provided courtside seats for a Lakers playoff game that night. The home team won, beating the San Antonio Spurs, and Kobe had 39 points wearing Jordans. The next day, there was a presentation at a Malibu mansion that overlooked the Pacific Ocean that the company had rented.

All the trappings were there. The slick presentation, the shoe mock-ups, and marketing concepts. But the game had been changed with that meeting at Reebok, just as Reebok hoped, and when the bottom line arrived there was a problem. The $100 million wasn't there. In the final paperwork from Adidas headquarters in Germany, the company had balked and offered significantly less guaranteed. There were incentives and royalty offerings that could have made it more than $100 million under certain circumstances, but the guarantee was for less than $60 million. Before Reebok, this would have been an awesome offer. After Reebok it didn't measure up. Everyone knew it. The air went out of the room. Vaccaro personally apologized to LeBron and his mother. He was crestfallen and demoralized not just because he knew he wasn't going to land LeBron but because he'd looked bad in the process, his bosses didn't back him up. He decided that day he was going to leave Adidas. Within two months he resigned. LeBron flew home thinking about Reebok and that $100 million.

The following Friday there was another private jet scheduled to come to Akron to get LeBron and family, this one belonging to Nike. It had been important for Nike to go last, they'd wanted it that way so that they could have a better control of the talks. But there are downsides to that strategy, especially because Nike had a certain way of doing business. They didn't like getting into bidding wars. Frequently they signed athletes for less than the competition was offering because of their superior product, branding, and marketing. Athletes wanted to be affiliated with Nike. Just a week before LeBron was due to come to town, Carmelo Anthony was on campus in Beaverton and his presentation, negotiation, and agreement to join Nike was wrapped up in one day.

But with the Reebok offer there, LeBron wanted some assurances before he made another long trip. He was talking to Merritt regularly but Merritt wasn't offering any number, just that LeBron would like what he heard. In truth, Merritt's job was to build a relationship and then sell the athlete on being with Nike, it wasn't to decide how much Nike could pay. The executives at Adidas evaluated things and decided that James didn't make sense financially at $100 million. The executives at Nike had some of the same research and had some of the same concerns.

For many years Nike's had a line in its annual report called "Demand Creation Expense." This is a catchall for their spending on endorsement deals, marketing, and advertising. Nike typically kept the number at about 11 or 12 percent of their revenue. Under that formula, for LeBron to be worth a $100 million endorsement deal Nike would like to believe his shoes and apparel would generate around $850 million in revenue during the term of the contract. That's a large business. When it came right down to it, Adidas CEO Herbert Hainer didn't like the chances. Phil Knight had to have a breaking point as well.

Not everything about an endorsement contract is so black-and-white. Nike sells cool and getting LeBron would be cool, which can't be quantified. For some perspective, Nike's budget for "demand creation" in 2003 was more than $1.2 billion (by 2017, it was $3.6 billion). While the company was chasing down these basketball free agents in the spring of 2003, it was also finishing up a deal to purchase rival shoe company Converse for $305 million, which it paid for in cash. Everything is relative. But for the LeBron portion of their business, Nike wanted him but didn't want to make a bad business deal.

With that as the backdrop, LeBron and his mom once again headed out to hear a pitch. Carter joined them, going back to Nike's campus. Because of school, LeBron didn't fly out until Friday afternoon. That meant the presentation was Saturday, which was unusual at Nike—they were typically on weekdays. It was at the Mia Hamm Building, a sleek new structure with tinted green windows that was the largest on the campus. Certain staples went into these things: special lighting, videos, products artfully displayed. But this one was the grandest Nike had done. It was put together by Wieden+Kennedy, the Portland creative agency that had designed most of Nike's great marketing efforts over the years. A poet was hired to read a work created for LeBron. There were examples of what his shoes could look like, what shirts and shorts and socks would be in his clothing line. One of the themes was LeBron as a lion, following the King James moniker he'd come to like. Some Nike executives estimated that between the merchandise and the man-hours, the company spent hundreds of thousands just on the pitch alone.

Then came time to talk. Normally, in these moments the agents would go into a conference room and the player would leave as the actual numbers and terms were presented. Goodwin was there and so was Fred Schreyer, a former lawyer for Nike who was then the commissioner of the Professional Bowlers Association but had been hired by Goodwin to assist in the negotiation. Nike was represented at the table by Ralph Greene and Adam Helfant, two of their top marketing executives.

But things started to go off script here. LeBron wanted to be there when the offer was actually made, which Nike wasn't prepared for. And he wanted Gloria to be there as well. After all, Reebok had them in the room when they made their offer and Reebok pulled out a $10 million check. LeBron, it seemed, was hoping for something just as grand. That wasn't how Nike did business. Knight had come to the presentation, and after his executives came to him with the issue, he said it was fine that LeBron and Gloria came into the conference room. This offer didn't draw any tears of joyful surprise out of the Jameses; it was for closer to $70 million guaranteed. As for the signing bonus, well, Nike had gotten word of the $10 million offer and they were prepared to do the same...sort of. They were not planning to have to tell this to LeBron directly, but the offer was for a $5 million bonus when he signed and then an additional $5 million as part of his paycheck later, once the long-form version of the deal was assembled. And there was no check on the table. Gloria didn't cry at that offer. All of the momentum that had built up during the presentation dissipated in a matter of moments.

To frame this offer, Tiger Woods's first deal at Nike was for $35 million. Bryant ended up agreeing to a $40 million deal with Nike that same year. What Nike put on the table was extremely impressive, just not as impressive as Reebok's offer. Further talks between the sides didn't go well. When the meeting broke and LeBron left campus, it didn't look like he was going to be wearing Nike. Several months earlier, a stock analyst at Merrill Lynch had put a buy rating on Nike under the assumption the company would sign LeBron. At the time, LeBron's lawyer put out a statement denying it, because he didn't want to kill the bidding war. The upshot is that Nike had some expectation they were going to make this deal; if they didn't land LeBron, then the stock price might've dropped if only temporarily.

That night, LeBron went to Merritt's house. Everyone knew things had gotten bleak. Merritt had a sinking feeling this would be his last meaningful time with LeBron. They ended up having a bit of a bonding session. LeBron befriended Merritt's teenage son, and they played video games together. Still, when Merritt saw LeBron off at the airport on Sunday, he didn't feel good about Nike's prospects.

Goodwin wanted to make a deal by the following Wednesday. The NBA's draft lottery was to be held that Thursday in New Jersey, the night LeBron would find out what team he'd be playing for the following season. It was possible LeBron could have gone to the New York Knicks, a huge market, or to the Memphis Grizzlies, one of the smallest markets. Goodwin didn't want market size to play into the bidding, and by setting this deadline, it encouraged the companies to make their best offers.

On Monday morning, employees at Nike came back to work expecting to get news that LeBron had agreed to sign over the weekend. More than one hundred employees played a role in the presentation, and some were eager to hear that they would be celebrating a win. Instead, when they stopped by the John McEnroe Building, where the marketing executive offices were, they found out the truth. As the finance guys said, "The delta between us and Reebok is significant." In other words, Nike was getting outbid, and it was getting worse. The door obviously wasn't shut, but the sides were stuck. Nike was ready to raise its offer, but it wanted Goodwin to make a counter first. Goodwin didn't want to counter. This little game dragged on for twenty-four hours with Merritt finally getting Goodwin to come off his position and make a counter, but they were still a long way from agreement.

Meanwhile, Goodwin remained in contact with Reebok, who smelled the chance to close. They increased their offer, eventually boosting it to more than $100 million. By the time the signing bonus and other factors were included, Reebok's offer to LeBron was around $115 million, according to those who were familiar with the final numbers—staggering. On that Tuesday, Reebok and Goodwin got close enough that plans were made for all the parties to fly to LeBron's hometown of Akron to try to formalize the contract. Reebok was going to make this happen. If they didn't think so, they wouldn't have sent executives and lawyers to Akron with paperwork.

While this was all playing out, LeBron became a millionaire. Goodwin put together LeBron's first endorsement deal with memorabilia and trading card maker Upper Deck, a multiyear package worth $6 million. Goodwin set up in a suite at the Radisson Hotel in downtown Akron, and when James signed, a representative from Upper Deck handed him a check for $1 million as a signing bonus. LeBron folded the check in half and put it in his pocket like it was routine, and then left to go back to school. All of this was happening as he was going through his last days of his senior year with his friends, days he wanted to cherish.

But LeBron had something else on his mind. He knew the numbers. He'd been sitting with the reality that he might be going with Reebok for a couple of weeks at that point. But he didn't want to do it. He didn't like their shoes that much. A couple of years earlier, one of Reebok's endorsers, Shawn Kemp, had said the shoes Reebok gave him failed during games, calling them "throwaways" in an interview with a newspaper reporter. Reebok sued Kemp for saying it, but he said it just the same. LeBron had always envisioned himself wearing Nike and wanted to be a part of their great ad campaigns and work with their designers.

Yet Reebok's offer was tens of millions more. That money was there to make LeBron forget about his hesitations. Nike certainly could have afforded to match the Reebok offer; it would have made little difference in their bottom line. But they had to do many more endorsement deals with many other athletes. They had to factor in holding that line to a degree. But when LeBron imagined his future, he'd always seen himself in Nikes. He'd dreamed of being in Nike commercials. He wanted to be like Jordan. He wanted to do business with Nike. In his words, he wanted to be in the Nike family. Some of it was Jordan's legacy. Some of it was superior branding. Some of it was ego: He wanted to wear the swoosh. Some of it was Merritt, who had been able to win LeBron's trust.

It was Wednesday. Reebok was in town, camping out in one room at the hotel ready to finish the deal. Goodwin called Nike back and more or less made it known that LeBron wanted to sign with them. If they improved their offer and agreed on a few points, they could get him. Helfant and Greene, the Nike executives, went into a frenzy, realizing they were back in the game. Knight was in New York at a funeral for Mark McCormack, the legendary sports agent, and got on the phone. He authorized an increased offer. As the Reebok executives waited, their counterparts at Nike put together a term sheet as evening approached. As they tried to finish, Knight was about to board his plane in New York to fly to his home in Palm Springs; he'd be out of touch for six hours.

After all that, LeBron agreed to a seven-year, $77 million guaranteed contract with Nike plus a $10 million signing bonus that would get the deal to $87 million. The Nike executives faxed the term sheet and said LeBron had to get it back as fast as possible. They waited by the fax machine, pacing, for the paper to come back with LeBron's signature. LeBron came to the hotel and didn't go to see the Reebok guys; instead, he went to Goodwin and Schreyer and signed one of the most important documents in his life.

Goodwin went down the hall to give the Reebok executives the news. They were furious about it all: Being used for leverage. Flying all the way in only to be left at the altar. Not being given a last chance to try to sweeten the deal. There were hard feelings all around.

For his part, Goodwin believes everything happened in good faith. He thought all along he was making the deal with Reebok. Like Steve Stoute, the former music executive who wanted to overwhelm James with an offer and finish the deal in a matter of moments, Goodwin had never seen anyone leave so much money on the table. Especially a teenager. Ultimately, Goodwin delivered what his client wanted: the most money they could squeeze out of Nike. It was actually even more than Knight had agreed to, and the Nike execs were a little worried about telling him the final number. When Knight landed, he called and was so thrilled they'd won that he never even mentioned it.

Over the long haul, LeBron ended up making significantly more on that deal once his royalties kicked in, pushing his earnings to over $100 million in that span. When the news went public—several outlets reported the deal as worth $90 million—it got massive attention in the basketball media, of course, but also on twenty-four-hour news shows and national newspapers. The number was so eye-popping, it became a cultural story. There was commentary on news shows and columns in editorial pages and the like. There was also reaction among NBA players. LeBron had just become the most highly paid shoe pitchman other than Jordan. He more than doubled Bryant's new deal, and Bryant was one of the faces of the league.

The following day, Reebok's stock dipped. It had leaked that week that they'd had the highest bid and there was some momentum that they'd win. The company felt the need to make a statement. It read: "While we believe LeBron James would have been a tremendous asset to Reebok, the costs associated with securing a long-term partnership with him was far beyond what we are willing to invest. Reebok's largest competitor simply put more money on the table and in the final hour—after carefully considering what is in the best interest of our business and our shareholders—Reebok elected to not match this offer...we feel great with what Reebok has achieved and that our recent string of unparalleled successes pressured our largest competitor into taking on this enormous cost."

This was extraordinary. A multinational corporation having to put out a statement about not signing a teenager to an endorsement contract. It was also not true: Reebok had offered more money. When they saw the news reports of the deal being worth $90 million, even if they weren't exactly accurate, the Reebok officials knew. They tweaked Nike anyway.

LeBron's partnership with Nike has had some ups and downs in the years since. But it's generally been a wonderful marriage. There have been a few tremendous marketing campaigns, including two giant billboards outside the Quicken Loans Arena in Cleveland that came to be trademarks in his career. LeBron so loved the first one, which read WE ARE ALL WITNESSES over a black-and-white photo of him, that he had the word *witness* tattooed on his leg. Both sides have made plenty of money along the way, LeBron earning hundreds of millions all told.

There was a certain amount of trust LeBron had to put in Nike back then: That they would support him even if he struggled early in his career. That they would feature him among their many athletes. That they would create shoes that not only looked good and would sell to the public but that he would actually like wearing. That they would put him in commercials that people would remember, like they did with Jordan.

In short, LeBron, a teenager who liked to wear backward baseball hats, tell off-color jokes, and hang out with friends, had to consider the long haul. Not because people were telling him it was important, but because he realized it was important. It's not something common for an eighteen-year-old to have to consider. For a teen who was about to be fabulously wealthy, taking the time to consider where he'd be at the end of the contract, much less at the end of his career, was a big ask.

Yes, LeBron picked Nike because he liked the company and thought it was cool. He picked them because it was what he saw Jordan wearing as a kid, and he wanted very much to be like his idol. He picked them because he believed they would put him in great commercials and design memorable campaigns. He picked them because he thought they could give him the best shoe designs. But he also picked them because, in that vital moment, he valued legacy over an all-out cash grab.

That showed a value system and an instinct that would end up setting the stage for many of the business decisions he made over the rest of his career.

A few years later, Reebok sold itself to Adidas. A few years after that, the Reebok basketball division was minimized. LeBron was more worried about legacy than some of the companies who were pitching him. That reality is lost in the details and the memories of all the money. But it may have been the most important takeaway of all.

That and the $10 million check that arrived by FedEx.

"Signing with Nike," LeBron said in 2018, "is the best business decision I've ever made."

# Chapter 4

# FOUR HORSES

The music was pounding so loudly that it was nearly impossible to hear the emcee as he bellowed into a microphone atop a temporary stage. Rotating colored lights danced across the walls and scantily clad young women strutted up and down a makeshift runway. One was wearing a T-shirt tied around her top to show off some sort of alternate way to use a piece of LeBron James Nike apparel, with the word *King* from a folded T-shirt wrapping around her chest.

As she turned to show off to the crowd, the knot at her back came loose. Whether it was an accident or wardrobe malfunction remains a mystery, but it gave the teenagers packed in next to the stage an unexpected show.

It was a mid-December night in North Philadelphia in 2003. A large shoe store along famed Broad Street had been transformed into a performance space as Nike picked this time and place to launch LeBron's first shoe, which it dubbed the Zoom Generation. It was a scattered and unfocused affair with the noise and darkness making it impossible to take it all in. Choosing Philly on a Thursday night in winter was some sort of weird message to Reebok and Allen Iverson, who owned that town at the time.

This was a symbolic moment in the first few years of LeBron's Nike association. He had plans to establish himself as both a brand and a basketball player, the sort of thing they talk about on panels at sports marketing conferences. There was lots of flash and plenty of excitement. There were some pretty awesome paychecks rolling in. But the execution was choppy.

After the massive Nike deal, agent Aaron Goodwin and LeBron turned their business attention to making a beverage endorsement decision. This was pretty standard. For star golfers, there were club endorsements and ball endorsements. For basketball stars, there were shoe deals and beverage deals. Like with the shoe contract, there were multiple bidders. The two biggest names in the industry, Pepsi and Coca-Cola, were interested in having LeBron as a pitchman.

Michael Jordan had been a long-term face for Pepsi and its Gatorade brand, which had the iconic "Be Like Mike" commercials in the mid-1990s. Gatorade also had a long-term relationship as the official sports drink sponsor of the NBA. It was on every NBA bench and every cup that players drank out of on the sidelines.

Coke had its own NBA deal with its Sprite brand as the official soda of the league. The company targeted kids and young adults with the brand, which made LeBron particularly attractive. Its signature event with the NBA was the Slam Dunk Contest over All-Star Weekend, which had Sprite branding all over it.

But there was another entrant, a company based in Queens, New York, called Glacéau, which made a product called VitaminWater. It was just a three-year-old brand in 2003 but had been growing quickly. It had more than $100 million in annual sales, which was impressive but paled in comparison to even Pepsi and Coke's smallest brands. In short, Glacéau couldn't offer the same type of endorsement cash that their bigger rivals could. The young company had positioned VitaminWater in health food markets and delis in and around New York and needed help breaking out of the mold of being a niche health product. They dreamed of LeBron's help in that regard, but it was a longshot.

Instead of offering a large guaranteed salary, they offered LeBron something they could give: a percentage of the company. If LeBron would be the face of the brand and help it grow, he would be in a position to greatly prosper. Glacéau believed in the power of influencer marketing. The company had done a deal with the New York Mets' David Wright, one of the most popular young athletes in New York at the time. Wright got 0.5 percent of VitaminWater to become a spokesman. The company was interested in making LeBron that type of partner. The final terms were never fully negotiated, but LeBron was being offered significantly more than Wright.

As the Nike deal proved, LeBron was already at the very top of the athlete endorsement game. Goodwin wanted to be selective, and LeBron had made it clear he wanted to make deals with companies he could be with for many years. He also wanted to pitch products he actually used. He wore Nikes. He drank Gatorade and Sprite. He didn't know VitaminWater. It was already the second-largest flavored water brand, but it was still just half the size of Pepsi's entrant in the market, a beverage called Propel. VitaminWater's future seemed bright, but it wasn't a sure thing. In a moment that would end up being instructive later, LeBron politely passed on the VitaminWater offer.

Coke made a positive impression in a meeting with Goodwin, making the largest endorsement offer to a player they'd ever made. Part of the pitch was Coke breaking from long-standing practice and being willing to make LeBron the face of two brands: Sprite and Powerade, their sports drink and rival to Gatorade. Right out of the gates, they presented a marketing concept to hype LeBron's first game and followed that with long-term plans with each brand that were appealing. It improved LeBron's position that Coke had sidelined its prime NBA spokesman, Kobe Bryant, because he was facing a rape allegation in Colorado. To help seal the deal, Coke invited LeBron to its Atlanta headquarters, where they held a rally in an auditorium—half of the room was wearing green to represent Sprite, and the other half wore blue to represent Powerade.

Regardless of what VitaminWater could offer, this pitch from one of the world's leading brands was too enticing. Goodwin put together a six-year deal that ended up being worth more than $20 million after LeBron reached some incentives. When that deal was over, he signed an eight-year extension, and then later extended it again. He's earned more than $40 million with the partnership, with more to come in the future. Like with Nike, it was a smart long-term choice with a premium partner that's paid off over the years.

LeBron's first television commercial was to pitch Sprite, a comical spot in which he scared his friends when he pretended to be cracking his neck in pain but actually was squishing an empty Sprite bottle behind his head. It featured a cameo by his friend Rich Paul, and is still one of the most memorable ads he's done.

He did run into an issue when he repeatedly declined to take part in the Slam Dunk Contest, which Sprite badly wanted him to do as title sponsor. It was especially a problem during his rookie season, when the event was held in Los Angeles. From the outset

LeBron had told Coke executives that he saw himself as an in-game dunker and not someone who would do well in a contest.

His feelings on the matter may have been influenced by a dunk contest in which he took part during his senior year in high school as part of the McDonald's All-American Game. LeBron won it, but it was tainted a little: He probably had been outperformed by Shannon Brown, a brilliant leaper who would later be LeBron's teammate on the Cavs. But the event was in Cleveland, and the judges gave him hometown scoring. If it had been L.A., it would've been without the hometown advantage and heavy expectations.

Sprite and Goodwin pushed LeBron hard to reconsider, and they presented him with a cool campaign idea where fans across the country would sign a petition to get him to take part. But LeBron said no as a rookie and every year after. Nonetheless, the relationship with Coke prevailed.

But about VitaminWater: A few months after LeBron passed, Glacéau did a major endorsement contract with the rapper Curtis Jackson, better known as 50 Cent. The company noticed Jackson drinking one of their products in a music video, and it spurred the relationship. The sides ended up cutting a deal that made Jackson an equity partner, as had been the offer to LeBron.

Three years later, thanks in part to a personalized

flavor created by Jackson called Formula 50 that helped the company grow, Coca-Cola bought VitaminWater for more than $4 billion.

Glacéau was a private company, so its records were kept private, but Jackson reportedly made between $60 and $100 million when he sold his shares as part of the deal. Wright also made millions. Meanwhile, by 2005, LeBron appeared in an ad for VitaminWater—playing a defense attorney whose mind was sharpened by drinking the product—as Coke shifted him away from pitching Powerade for a period.

It's worth pointing out that 50 Cent was in a different position from LeBron. Coke and Pepsi weren't coming after him, trying to sign him. He wasn't turning down millions to gamble on a little engine that could. But his willingness to attach his name to the brand ended up creating an incredible payday.

For LeBron, not getting the same deal wasn't about jealousy—50 Cent later filed for bankruptcy—it was a learning experience. At the time, as a teenager, LeBron enjoyed the idea of being paid millions to be the voice of something. What happened with VitaminWater and 50 Cent would have been an interesting case study for LeBron even if the company hadn't approached him with an offer. It was a lesson about the difference between being an employee and being an owner in a brand. It showed that taking a calculated risk on a young company could pay off, especially if that company was so desperate to attach itself to LeBron's brand power that it was willing to give up potentially valuable ownership shares.

In a way, LeBron was an "owner" of his Nike brand. Athletes who have their own signature shoes with Nike often get 5 percent of gross sales as a royalty. A certain payout is guaranteed—LeBron was getting $11 million per year from Nike starting in 2003 before his signature shoe sold a single pair—and then the athlete would collect additional money if sales passed the guarantee. But that isn't the same as ownership in a company, obviously. Had LeBron gotten 5 percent of Nike when it was a startup, it would be quite a different story. Of course, finding the next big thing—a VitaminWater, for example—can be hard. But those opportunities were out there and worth looking for.

It was part of an awakening LeBron had after he reached his twentieth birthday. As he was getting settled with the Cavs, his close friends took positions around him. As planned, Nike indeed made Maverick Carter a full-time job offer to work on LeBron's products at a healthy six-figure salary.

Randy Mims, who had been close to LeBron's surrogate father, Eddie Jackson, and took on a helping role when Jackson went to prison, became LeBron's right-hand man. Mims is ten years older than LeBron and quiet, though people who know him enjoy his sense of humor. His title was "road manager" in a company

LeBron formed called King James Inc. But essentially Mims's job was to make sure LeBron had whatever he needed around games and when he traveled. Sometimes, after making sure LeBron was set up for a game, Mims would leave the arena and take a commercial flight to the next city and meet the team when it came in hours later. Eventually, the Cavs just let Mims start flying on the team charter. In 2005, they hired him to a full-time position called "player liaison."

Rich Paul met LeBron at Akron-Canton Airport when LeBron was in high school. LeBron admired a high-end Warren Moon throwback jersey Paul was wearing. Paul, who is four years older than LeBron, had a little business in throwback jerseys, which were popular at the time. Paul would fly down to Atlanta, where there was a supplier he knew, buy them, and bring them home to sell essentially out of his trunk. LeBron was very much into throwback jerseys.

He was suspended for a game in high school for accepting two free throwbacks in exchange for taking a photo at a store near Cleveland, a mini-scandal that revealed the high school sports governing body's difficulty in dealing with his phenomenon.

Allow me to take a little detour here: The hypocrisy of punishing LeBron for taking some free stuff when he was generating hundreds of thousands of dollars was both short-sighted and shameful. Most of his games were moved to larger venues so more tickets could be sold, and all of the games sold out. He even sold out Gund Arena (now Quicken Loans Arena) in Cleveland, more than 20,000 seats, in one game in his senior year when the Cavs were dead last in the NBA in attendance at less than 12,000 per game. Several of his games were on national television, others were on regional television, and some were on pay-per-view.

Because of an agreement with Adidas, LeBron was wearing free shoes and uniforms so that the logo would be seen on him in all TV clips and photos. Promoters were guaranteeing payouts and covering expenses to fly his team to games in North Carolina, New Jersey, Delaware, and California. This was all deemed to be fine. But a couple of jerseys so the owner of a little shop could put his photo on the wall was considered taboo.

Within a couple of days of the suspension, LeBron hired one of the best attorneys in Cleveland, and he quickly won a court battle to get reinstated after a one-game suspension. The athletic association's bylaws weren't written to withstand anything like him—a first-year law student could have identified that. It probably wasn't even entirely the association's fault; they were getting so many jealous complaints from other schools that they got to the point where they threw up their hands.

Earlier the governing body had to perform an investigation as to how LeBron was able to get a brand-new Hummer H2 vehicle that was customized and likely cost more than $70,000. It was quickly discovered that a bank was eager to give Gloria James a fully legitimate loan for the car. Considering her son was a virtual lock to become a millionaire in a matter of months and would need a place to deposit the checks, the institution saw her as a safe risk. The bankers had more perspective and understanding than the school administrators did. But let's move on.

That day at the airport, LeBron told Paul about two jerseys he'd been coveting: a gold Magic Johnson throwback and a Joe Namath throwback from when he played for the L.A. Rams. Paul tracked them down for him within a few days. That transaction ended up as the start of a long friendship. Paul believes his choice to wear that Moon throwback that day—he had considered a polo shirt instead—changed his life.

Paul became the second employee of King James Inc. Paul was from a rough neighborhood in Cleveland but had also attended a private Catholic high school, where he was in the minority. He and LeBron were able to connect on several levels. One of the roles he took on was planning for-profit parties where LeBron would make appearances. It was a cottage industry in the NBA in the early and mid-2000s. A player like LeBron could get tens of thousands of dollars for being at an event. Organizers could charge large cover fees for guests who wanted to simply attend the same party as star players. If you wanted to get into the VIP area, where the celebrities actually were, that came at a premium. LeBron began attending these events in big cities like New York, Chicago, Los Angeles, Miami, and Washington, DC, when the Cavs had off nights, or even sometimes after games when the team had flown in. After he turned twenty-one, he was able to do it at higher-end nightclubs.

LeBron was comfortable with this group. They were young, they were loyal, and he had total confidence in them. One thing was for sure: They were making money. They started to call each other the Four Horsemen. To cement this moniker, they had clothing and jewelry made to commemorate their bond. Carter and Paul often sat in courtside seats; LeBron seemed to be comforted by their presence on the road.

Shortly after landing his Nike deal and getting his signing bonus, LeBron bought a large estate just outside Akron for about $1 million. He wanted a place where he could have a 100-yard football field to play flag football with friends. He got it, even if he would later tear down the house and rebuild a giant mansion in its place. But in addition to that, LeBron rented an apartment in Cleveland in an upscale building for nights when he didn't want to drive forty-five minutes back home and where he could spend time on game days. He ended up sharing the same hallway as Wes Wesley, who continued to spend time in Cleveland to be with Dajuan Wagner.

Wesley didn't help Reebok get LeBron, but that wasn't the end of the relationship. It was more like a beginning. Wesley had played this role, helping young players adjust to the NBA, for many years, and he began doing the same with LeBron and his group of friends. Nike had bought four floor seats to Cavs games near the team bench—Phil Knight came to LeBron's first home game and sat in them—and Merritt also used them when he was in town. But on many nights Wesley was in them. Yes, he'd worked with Reebok a few months earlier, but he was the ultimate free agent. He moved from entity to entity, depending on what jobs needed to be done and what opportunities presented themselves.

As LeBron moved through his first two years in the NBA, he began to feel some growing pains with his actions off the floor. His life changed during training camp of his second year when his longtime girlfriend, Savannah Brinson, gave birth to a son. He named him LeBron Jr. The Cavs were having training camp at Capital University in Columbus. Savannah was overdue and scheduled to give birth the next day. LeBron had to explain why he would miss some practice time, so it was arranged for me to interview him under a set of bleachers after an evening practice.

"I didn't have a father," LeBron said that night. "I'm going to make sure I give everything to my son that I didn't have."

Years later, LeBron would say he regretted giving his first son his name because it put pressure on him. It was a sign of how his views matured and adjusted over the years. But on that night in October 2004, it was meaningful to him. Nonetheless, it was a time of adjustment. And one of the things he thought about was how he operated his business.

Goodwin and his brother and partner, Eric, had helped put together nearly $150 million in endorsement deals. In addition to Nike, Coke, and Upper Deck, there had been a $5 million deal with Cadbury Schweppes to market their Bubblicious line of gum that included LeBron's first Super Bowl commercial. It was already perhaps the most impressive portfolio of any active NBA player and certainly the best ever achieved by a teenager. *Sports Illustrated* profiled Goodwin, setting up a photo with LeBron lounging on a couch and Goodwin standing behind him... the guy behind the guy.

Dwight Howard, the number one overall pick in the 2004 NBA draft, decided to pick him to be his agent as well.

At the same time, Goodwin could be demanding. A veteran agent with plenty of experience working with young pros, it was his preference to limit access of friends and associates to the player's business deals. Goodwin didn't like LeBron entering into side deals with his close friends. He discouraged some of the for-profit parties that LeBron's friends used to generate money.

LeBron's friends didn't see the problem; if they wanted to go to a club to enjoy themselves, the club would often benefit from them going there. There were internet sites that alerted users when and where famous athletes and entertainers liked to party. An economy was built around it. The Four Horsemen saw a window where they could take advantage and at least be able to get a share. LeBron was far from alone in being on this circuit; big-name players were in demand.

Perhaps more important, Goodwin was wary of Wesley spending so much time around his top client. Wesley had a long association with agent Leon Rose, and Goodwin suspected that Wesley's relationship building with LeBron and his inner circle had ulterior motives. None of this, it must be said, is unusual for NBA players or the player-agent relationship. It's a world of sharks where agents who complain about clients being poached often troll for new clients as well.

At one point, Goodwin and the group had a bit of a blowup over an event in Toronto. One of Goodwin's high-profile clients, Gary Payton, had been arrested at a club there, and Goodwin suspected it was part of a setup (Payton was later acquitted of the charges). Goodwin didn't want LeBron to attend. LeBron went anyway.

As this was playing out, Wesley had been talking to LeBron, Carter, Mims, and Paul about the value he thought they could bring to other athletes. Wesley's friendship with Jay-Z helped deepen LeBron's connection to the star. LeBron's hero as a kid was Michael Jordan, but as he developed as an adult, it was Jay-Z he started to feel a connection to. Not just because of the music, which he loved, but also how Jay-Z branched out.

Jay-Z took control of his management. He did straight pitches—selling everything from high-end watches to beer to computers—but he also created businesses. He had his own record label, his own clothing line. Eventually he had his own sports representation agency and music-streaming service. He made millions selling songs, but he made tens of millions becoming an influencer and attaching his name to help sell brands. When Jay-Z regularly attended games in New York and Los Angeles, these were the things they talked about. And Wesley was often there, offering ways to help LeBron go in that direction.

On the floor, LeBron's career was off to a good start. He'd won Rookie of the Year in 2004 and in his second season he was voted as an All-Star starter by the fans. He was ubiquitous on television advertising and had become a draw for national television games. His team wasn't yet successful—they missed the playoffs his first two seasons and fired coach Paul Silas—but they were improving. Things were generally going well.

As his second season came to a close, Maverick Carter and LeBron began talking about what it would be like if they opened up their own marketing firm. When he became a top face in the music world, Jay-Z started working with other artists. Could LeBron do the same?

Carter had spent two years at Nike studying how it operated sports marketing. Merritt had become more than a brand manager for LeBron's shoes; he'd quickly developed into a mentor for both Carter and LeBron. Merritt opened doors for Carter in Beaverton. He could have been a token employee given an ancillary job as a side deal. But he was serious about learning, and Merritt respected that. As one of the most powerful people on campus, he enabled Carter to grow there. Though Carter hadn't graduated from college, he believed he'd gotten what amounted to a degree from studying at the "University of Nike," a line he would use many times over the years to help establish his qualifications.

During one night at Carter's mother's house back in Akron, the two sat down and plotted out how a new company might look. NBA agents' commissions were capped at 4 percent and often were negotiated downward for the bigger stars on larger contracts. But for marketing deals, the broker often got commissions as high as 10–15 percent. It was a hard business to crack and even harder to excel in. But with LeBron as a client and as a possible recruiter for others, there was a chance of creating something. This was one of the lessons LeBron had already learned, how influence could be monetized if handled correctly.

The plan was audacious on its face. The concept that a

twenty-five-year-old with no college degree and limited secondhand experience could handle a multimillion-dollar business like LeBron was ripe for mockery. Magic Johnson, who has been one of the most successful basketball players–turned–businessmen of all time, has had a general rule that he doesn't make investments with people who are going into business with family or friends. It seemed like a classic and youthful mistake.

Though Goodwin was wary of how their relationship was going, he was still surprised when LeBron called with the news he was going in a different direction. It caught me and many others who were around him off guard, too. It wasn't that everyone didn't know LeBron harbored grand plans for his business operations. It was that this seemed like a misstep for a young man who had done almost everything right.

Those who knew Carter liked him, and he'd won the respect of those he was in business with. But to be the face of LeBron's off-court operations and to represent him at meetings with Fortune 500 companies and at major functions was naturally looked at with skepticism at best and mockery at worst. Perhaps if all of them had been a little older, it would have been more accepted, but this seemed like an unnecessary risk from a young player. Regardless of some rough edges at the time, Goodwin had delivered LeBron generally excellent results. I knew that Goodwin had lost some big-name clients over the years, namely Paul Pierce and Jason Kidd. He eventually lost Howard and later got and lost megastar Kevin Durant. He made big deals for all of them along the way, but his demanding ways seemed to wear on his clients. Changing agents is routine for players, but this move was still mildly shocking at the time.

Though there were some initial hard feelings, Goodwin and LeBron maintained a generally positive relationship in the years after the parting. Whatever minor issues existed, it wasn't entirely personal. Goodwin was right about one thing, though. If LeBron was going to let Carter lead future marketing deals, he needed a certified agent to handle his basketball deals. He was eligible for his first contract extension just a year later. In the end he hired Rose, Wesley's longtime partner. Wesley offered good advice and connections, but he was a businessman, too. He closed that deal.

When the big move became public, the reaction was severe, especially when neither LeBron nor Carter seemed to have a strategy for how to explain their plans to the media. When pressed, they asked to be given a few months before they'd explain what their plans were. This was a reasonable position to take, but it didn't stop some intense short-term judgment. The working title of their venture, Four Horsemen Management, didn't land well with critics, either. It made for open season on the media front. LeBron was heavily ripped, probably more harshly than for anything he'd done on the floor during his young career.

It didn't help perception that a year earlier the show *Entourage* had premiered on HBO, featuring a young Hollywood star, his three friends, and their missteps as they tried to leverage their careers alongside his. The show was a hit. And the headlines comparing the Four Horsemen to the *Entourage* characters wrote themselves (LeBron later made a guest appearance on the show, completing the circle). There may have been some racial tension at play here, with many older white journalists and commentators judging the concept of four young black men being able to run a delicate business. But there was plenty of grounded commentary questioning the choice, too.

One cutting column contained a line that irked the four friends for years. It read, "A few years from now, when LeBron needs knee surgery, he'll have his plumber do the job." There were many more like it.

However, a few respected voices came out in their defense. One of them was Sonny Vaccaro. Gone from Adidas and now working with Reebok, Vaccaro was willing to accept interview requests and defend and vouch for Carter. So did some other executives who had experience dealing with him. No matter what the assumptions were, those who actually had spent time with Carter were impressed by him. He didn't like to do business in the morning—he was well known for sleeping late—and he wasn't always on time. These were signs of youth. But when it came time to talk about deals, Carter continually proved to be thoughtful and careful. He didn't strike people as seeking instant gratification. He was someone who said no more frequently than yes, even on chances to put money in his pocket. That alone should have proven this wasn't some sort of bad cliché, but those details weren't as publicized.

When he was in high school and people chided him for some of his decisions, LeBron had no issue focusing on the long game. Part of the reason he left Goodwin was because he sensed a stagnation. He knew he could get endorsement deals and could pitch products. But he wanted to expand his horizons. Even at age twenty, he had a sense that he'd have to be a little uncomfortable to expand his empire.

"I knew I had to grow as a businessperson," LeBron said. "So why not let the guys around me grow with me? We can all see our mistakes. Let's get in the bunker together."

After taking a few months to plan, the group debuted a new name: LRMR Marketing. It was the initials of their first names—LeBron, Randy, Maverick, and Rich—and it had a cool logo and a sleek website with lots of impressive verbiage. They still didn't have a business beyond LeBron, but at least they were able to articulate their vision in a way that created a modicum of respect. Had they had this ready when they made the break from

Goodwin, it would have probably dramatically softened the blow. But that was just part of the learning process. They opened an office in Cleveland and got to work.

But there was more than just a nameplate and a nice façade: They had a plan. It was as complicated as it was brave. And they were determined to pull it off.

# Chapter 5

# FAILING UP

The signs were posted on the doors, above the benches, and even outside the locker room. No agents were allowed on the premises; this was a designated safe space for amateurs only. Maverick Carter, a fully engaged marketing agent, would sit comfortably below these warnings as he watched scrimmages at the University of Akron's Rhodes Arena.

Rhodes Arena is hardly impressive, an aging multipurpose facility that lacks charm or glamour. But it is a home of sorts to LeBron James. He played many high school basketball games there, his popularity forcing his team out of their small home gym. Keith Dambrot, LeBron's first high school coach, was later the head coach at Akron for thirteen years, and he made sure LeBron always had the building at his disposal.

For a number of years in the late 2000s, every

July Nike took the building over for what it called the LeBron James Skills Academy. In 2006, Nike ended its signature summer event for elite high school players, the All-American Camp, which it had held for years in Indianapolis. The replacement was this camp built around LeBron. It turned the midsummer event into a supercharged recruiting festival. And it was a pillar in LeBron and Carter's plans to become a serious player in the representation and player dealmaking business.

Nike invited top players from its affiliated AAU teams as well as those who had been standouts at other position-focused camps around the country. But there was another layer that added value. Many of the top college players in the country were invited to come and work as "counselors" to the high school campers. As a result, in this college gym in Ohio, dozens of up-and-comers from both high school and college levels would gather in one place and be hosted by LeBron.

It set the stage for an exciting and competitive environment. After drills and some scrimmaging, the college stars would drop their counselor façade and play pickup games against each other. Some of the top high school players would mix in with the games. Then, when the time was right, LeBron would enter and play with the top guys in camp. These pickup games probably wouldn't have been possible in any other setting and left some lasting memories.

In 2009, a college player from Xavier University

named Jordan Crawford had a tremendous dunk with LeBron defending him. It was a cool moment for Crawford, who was drafted in the first round the next year. It became famous when Lynn Merritt asked for the videotape of the moment from a film crew that had captured it. It made it seem like Nike was trying to protect LeBron from being embarrassed. It was no big deal; another tape surfaced anyway and showed Crawford had made a great and memorable play.

One year, the high school roster had future All-Stars DeMar DeRozan and DeMarcus Cousins as well as future Rookie of the Year Tyreke Evans. And the college counselors included future pros Ty Lawson, Wesley Matthews, and twins Brook and Robin Lopez. Another year, future All-Stars Klay Thompson and Kemba Walker plus Chandler Parsons were there as counselors, and one of the campers was future number one overall pick Anthony Davis. Dozens of other players who ended up as major college talents and NBA draft picks came through the camp over the years.

It was a first-class event that included a high-end banquet, where LeBron would get even more face time with the young players. Sometimes there would be more private meetings at LeBron's home. By the end of the week, he'd often established relationships with some of the top players. He might see some at his camp two or three times by the time they entered the draft. It was all part of the Nike machine aimed at recruiting the top players and trying to ensure they would be wearing Nikes when they became pros.

But it was also part of a multistage plan that LeBron, Carter, Merritt, and even Wesley were involved in. It was actually rather shrewd. The group was leveraging young players' affinity for LeBron and using his status as one of the game's top players to create a way to get in on the ground floor. It was certainly in a gray area, with LeBron essentially running his own marketing firm, making him a de facto agent, and having free access to all these high school and college players. NCAA rules can be vague and sometimes even ridiculous, but even that regulation labyrinth didn't have a clear case file to cover this situation. So LeBron and LRMR Marketing pretty much ignored it, and the NCAA essentially looked the other way.

Numerous agents dance with the rules to establish inroads with young players. There's a culture of runners who feed agents and financial planners who are often tied into the process as well. In 2018, a federal case was made against a former Adidas employee who leveraged relationships with college coaches to influence where top prospects went to school. In that case, it was the University of Louisville, though numerous other schools were tied up in the probe. It's a reality in the basketball world, a world LeBron had to move through and learn from. So LRMR, Nike, and Wesley working together to get to amateur athletes wasn't the cleanest operation when looked at through the lens of what the NCAA says is right and wrong. But that's not the real world, and everyone knew it.

In a perfect scenario, this is how it would go: Nike would identify the player and get him in their elite camps. LeBron would get to know the player. The player would turn pro and pick LRMR to do his marketing and Leon Rose to be his agent, and Nike would sign him to an endorsement contract. There was also one more facet, which involved Wesley: Ideally the player would go to play for John Calipari or another of the college coaches Wesley had a relationship with. Wesley and Calipari, though, were especially close. Milt Wagner, Wesley's lifelong friend, joined Calipari's coaching staff at the University of Memphis when Dajuan Wagner went there for a year, one of many mutually beneficial arrangements that flowed out of Wesley's partnerships over the years.

Wesley played a role in Evans—who is from Wesley's home territory in Philadelphia—ending up going to Memphis to play for Calipari and signing with Nike. So did another of Wesley's "nephews," Chris Douglas-Roberts, who also attended the LeBron Skills Academy, went to Memphis, and signed with Rose to be his agent. Wesley was clearly guiding players to Calipari but with such charisma and magnetism behind the scenes that no one seemed to care. At one point the *New York*

*Times* reported that Jim Delany, the commissioner of the Big Ten Conference and a former NCAA investigator himself, told Wesley that he'd love it if he could start sending some of his valuable players to Big Ten schools. Considering the high level of hypocrisy within the NCAA, this was par for the course. At the end of the day in this murky world, one thing was clear: Wesley was helping kids navigate it and benefit from it as much as possible.

As this operation was churning along, a special case came into focus: a talented, muscular, and super quick guard from Chicago named Derrick Rose. He was a big-time talent that Nike, Wesley, and Calipari all wanted. LRMR would have loved to be involved, too. Derrick's brother, Reggie Rose, kept most agent runners and even college coaches away from Derrick in an effort to protect him. But one who got through was Wesley, who had a relationship with Michael Jordan that earned him credibility in Chicago. Sure enough, Derrick ended up at Memphis and with Calipari led the team to 38 wins and a heartbreaking defeat in the 2008 NCAA title game. All of that was later forfeited because of chicanery around his SAT score, which mysteriously was taken in Detroit by someone who was not Derrick Rose, the NCAA decided.

Nike had set up Reggie Rose with an excellent job running a grassroots basketball program in Chicago. Wesley had worked his magic. Rose had been awesome under Calipari and he was headed for the number one overall pick, which serendipitously was won by his hometown Chicago Bulls, and eventually a signature shoe with an eight-figure endorsement contract. It's no wonder there'd been so much positioning and even cheating to get aligned with Rose, he was that special of a prospect.

But then there was a curveball. Derrick Rose didn't pick Leon Rose to represent him; he went with agent Arn Tellem instead. And he didn't sign with Nike; he took a huge deal with Adidas and soon became the face of their basketball product. Reggie Rose got a six-figure consulting deal with Adidas, which also agreed to bankroll the Rose family AAU team in Chicago. LRMR, it goes without saying, didn't get to become the marketing agent.

This was a setback on a number of fronts. LRMR wasn't off to a flying start. Carter did put together a few deals for LeBron. One was with lawnmower maker Cub Cadet, a Cleveland-based company that was the Cavs' largest sponsor. It was a multimillion-dollar deal, but it wasn't in the same league as those Goodwin had put together. The more significant pact was with Microsoft, one of the largest brands in the world. The first activation had LeBron appear briefly in a television ad for the company's Vista operating system plus launching a website aimed at kids. The website was announced at a splashy event at a community center in Las Vegas at the 2007 All-Star Weekend. It was the first time Microsoft had ever done a deal with an NBA player, and it seemed like the type of innovative arrangement Carter and LeBron had envisioned when they started the company.

However, it wasn't a good partnership, and it fizzled. The Microsoft executive who put the deal together left the company, and Microsoft ended the deal within two years. LRMR had signed two other clients in that span, but neither of them were NBA players. One was Ted Ginn Jr., a wide receiver in the NFL, and the other was Mike Flynt, a fifty-nine-year-old who made headlines when he played a season of college football at a small school in West Texas. Ginn never got a significant marketing deal; doing so is a real challenge for NFL players who aren't superstars. LRMR had big plans for Flynt, including a movie. The movie never happened, and Carter ended up helping to put together a book deal. LeBron wrote the foreword.

There were issues with the deals that were in place, too, including at Nike. LeBron's product wasn't performing all that well; its growth had been slower than Nike had hoped. Nike had only a handful of employees working on the brand full-time for a while, though they did boost the staffing in 2007 when LeBron made a huge splash by leading the Cavs to an unexpected run to the Finals. It included a breathtaking upset of the Pistons in the conference finals, including a double overtime game in which LeBron scored 29 of the Cavs' final 30 points.

But by 2008 Tinker Hatfield, Nike's legendary shoe designer, stopped working with LeBron because he said he was tired of dealing with those around him. Hatfield had been the main designer of LeBron's shoes, but he left to work on Kobe Bryant's shoe line and Jordan Brand projects.

"I don't like working with LeBron's entourage," Hatfield said at a promotional event at a shoe store in 2010. "It's too many people, too many ideas, too many opinions."

At another event a few months later, Hatfield said LeBron's designs had "suffered a little bit" and hadn't "done as well as the Kobe stuff."

"Working with Kobe, one guy comes into the room with him and he has ideas and is very forward thinking and is smart about what he needs to do, what he thinks he needs to do to be a better player," Hatfield said. "LeBron is a great guy, I really like him, but when he comes into the room and he's got like eight other guys saying things. That is one reason why the LeBron stuff, even though it does OK, it isn't quite as exciting to me as the Kobe stuff or what we've done with the Jordan Brand."

Creative differences are commonplace in the shoe design business, and LeBron had his ups and downs with Nike. One year during his annual meeting with designers in Oregon, LeBron expressed frustration with what was being made for him; Phil Knight, who was in the room, snapped at some of his employees on LeBron's behalf. Another year, LeBron was so upset by the performance of that year's signature model that he stopped wearing it and switched to an older, more comfortable version. But there were plenty of years when LeBron was thrilled with the design and special colorways that were created for him, such as Christmas Day shoes.

But by 2009, two things happened that promised to boost business. Creative Artists Agency, the Hollywood talent juggernaut, decided to enter the athlete representation business. To get started, CAA purchased a number of smaller agencies to build up a client base across the major sports. Leon Rose's NBA practice was one of them, linking the operation to a major brand. Wesley eventually became an agent at CAA himself, representing coaches. One of his first clients was, not surprisingly, Calipari.

The other big event was Calipari getting hired as the coach at the University of Kentucky, instantly making him one of the most powerful coaches in the world of basketball. Calipari running one of the biggest programs in the country opened up huge opportunities for LeBron and his group. He wasted no time in trying to leverage the situation.

LeBron accepted an invitation to speak to the

Kentucky players prior to Calipari's first season and to reconnect with a couple of his former camp attendees: Cousins and a super talented freshman from North Carolina named John Wall. With Rose off in the NBA with the Bulls, Wall had replaced him both as Calipari's point guard and the next star-in-waiting that agents were obsessed with signing. Cousins, also expected to be a high pick, wasn't far behind. But it was Wall, a dynamic speed demon, who had the best chance to land a major shoe deal and potentially pass down millions in commissions to agents. After Rose had slipped through their fingers, Nike and LeBron revved up their chase to make sure they got the expected number one overall pick this time.

LeBron started praising Wall in the media and wearing Kentucky gear to games. He even flew down to Lexington to see the Wildcats play a game in January of that year, a victory over Vanderbilt, and led cheers on court during a timeout. After the game, he visited Calipari and the team in the locker room. This seemed like an odd step to the casual observer. LeBron had been closely associated with Ohio State's basketball program for years. In 2007, the Buckeyes became the first school to wear LeBron's personal Nike logo on their uniforms. Ohio State was still wearing his signature shoes as a team every game in the 2009–10 college season.

Yet here was LeBron down in Kentucky wearing its blue and white and dancing at midcourt. He was there to support Calipari, who had become a friend through Wesley. But the basis of all of it was Wall. LeBron was hoping he could be a signature young athlete to add to his marketing firm's clientele. As for Calipari, if Rose and Wall both moved on and got drafted at the top of the draft and then landed big-time endorsements, it would only help him continue to get the top high school prospects in the nation to come to Kentucky. Nike and Wesley were out there looking for them.

Wall had a great season, averaging 17 points and seven assists a game on a team loaded with future NBA players like Cousins, Eric Bledsoe, Patrick Patterson, and Daniel Orton. The Wildcats went 35-3, losing in the Elite Eight. Just like with Rose, Wall became the number one overall pick in the draft. And like with Rose, LeBron and his friends and business partners missed out on the deals completely. Wall passed on LeBron and LRMR and instead hired agent Dan Fegan. He also passed on Nike, signing a five-year, $25 million deal with Reebok.

Years later, Carter told me one of his biggest mistakes was chasing other athletes to manage, like Wall. Not because he wasn't able to land any major basketball stars—Carter did briefly manage NFL quarterback Johnny Manziel and helped him get a seven-figure Nike deal before Manziel's career fell apart because of excessive partying—but because it was a waste of time. Carter had to fight several battles when making these huge swings for big stars. First, he had to sell that he could do big deals for someone other than LeBron. Carter, at that point, had a limited reputation. The other was that the athletes Carter tried to recruit weren't sure they would be the priority. How could LeBron not always be first when it came to business opportunities? These players loved LeBron and enjoyed the relationship, but when it came time to make such an important decision, Carter was at a disadvantage.

As an athlete marketing company, LRMR was a failure. But by the time Wall made his choices on representation and which shoes to wear, LeBron, Carter, and Rich Paul had started to make a pivot.

# Chapter 6

# CAMERAMAN

It was just boilerplate language on a single sheet of paper, a basic release that all students in the documentary film class at Loyola Marymount University had to get subjects to sign to take part in the semester-long project they all had to turn in. One day after school at St. Vincent–St. Mary in the spring of 2003, Kristopher Belman got LeBron James and several of his friends and teammates to sign them at a secretary's desk just off the gym. In his mind, Belman was just checking off a box to satisfy his professor. He had no idea how much those signatures would end up being worth or the power it would end up giving him.

Belman was from Akron and a couple of years older than LeBron. He and I grew up one block apart in a middle-class neighborhood on the west side of town. We went to the same elementary school, though he was younger. His dad was my flag football coach one year. He was a big sports fan but even more into filmmaking. He went to film school in California. When I saw him turn up on the sidelines and in the huddles at LeBron's games wearing a black hat and dark clothes and holding a video camera, I had no idea what was going on. I hadn't seen him in years. He hadn't gone to St. Vincent–St. Mary; he went to high school at rival Walsh Jesuit.

Belman was in the right place at the right time. With so many trying to get access to LeBron and his team in their senior year—not to mention the agent Joe Marsh, who had been planning a multimillion-dollar documentary himself—the team was turned off somewhat to established media. LeBron, in his opinion, had been burned by a less-than-flattering feature in *ESPN the Magazine* and had curtailed his one-on-one interviews. With national outlets swarming following his brief suspension midway through his senior season, both LeBron and the school had tired of requests and began to turn almost everything down. The most extensive interview LeBron gave during the season was, oddly enough, to NFL Hall of Famer Deion Sanders for *The Early Show* on CBS.

But Belman was a neutral figure, a young man with a seemingly pure agenda. He got a request to the team's head coach, Dru Joyce, and was able to get a surprising yes. Joyce, it turned out, said no to most of the pros and yes to the college student. And so there was Belman on the bus, in the hotels, and in the locker rooms as one of the highest-profile teams in high school basketball history made their way toward the culmination of LeBron's high school career. It turned out to be a traumatic last few weeks of the season, with LeBron's brief suspension and a close call in the state championship game.

When it was over, Belman had one hell of a class project—and hours and hours of footage that no one else had. Long after the class was over, Belman realized he had something of real value and pondered just what he could do with these tapes. LeBron was off to the NBA with a huge Nike contract and on his way to being Rookie of the Year, fast developing into one of the most interesting athletes in American sports. All of the major media outlets had produced major features about him. There was such interest in this new face in the NBA that newspapers routinely sent reporters out to Cavs games before LeBron arrived in town so they could prepare stories ahead of time. And here was Belman with all of this unseen footage sitting at his apartment near LAX.

He would listen to the audio of the tapes on his way to and from class. He watched them over and over to the point that he had the dialogue memorized. He'd dreamed up storyboards for what a feature-length project might look like. He didn't have his degree yet, but he had this footage he could have sold to HBO or ESPN if he had wanted to or had he known about Marsh, who was preparing to sue LeBron for millions because he didn't get the stuff Belman had captured for free. It could have netted him a beautiful profit on a straight sale. He had the releases. He owned the film free and clear. He didn't have to involve LeBron or anyone else in where it ended up.

But Belman didn't want a check. He wanted to make a real film, one that he could put his name on as director. One that could help launch his career. He looked for a way to make it happen, taking meeting after meeting and repeatedly failing to make a connection with a producer who wanted to bankroll the project with him as the director. Lots of people wanted to buy the footage from him, especially when they learned LeBron had signed away any ownership. But no one trusted him with it. Belman was working at a coffee shop. Years went by, and the interest in LeBron's high school years waned as he became a star in the league.

Four years later, in 2007, Belman was out of school and a struggling artist living among other struggling artists in L.A. He realized he needed what he once prized not needing: LeBron's involvement. If he could come to a producer with LeBron as a partner, it could change everything. The problem was, Belman didn't have a relationship with LeBron. Yes, LeBron remembered him, but he'd long since moved on. Honestly, he wasn't even sure if LeBron knew his name. He always had just called him "cameraman."

Belman had an idea to try to recapture LeBron's attention. He put together an eleven-minute sizzle reel of his footage, culminating in the victory that clinched that mythical national title and represented a full circle for that team after they'd lost in the state title game the season before. That was really the story; it wasn't so much about LeBron's senior season as it was about the four other seniors rebounding from that letdown. Belman was able to show the reel to several of LeBron's former high school teammates, including Romeo Travis. He'd kept in touch with Travis and some of the other people from the team, but he hadn't talked to LeBron in years. Back in Akron for a few days over the summer, he asked Travis for a favor: Could he please show the DVD to LeBron?

Belman waited for a week and nothing happened. It was almost time for him to fly back to L.A. At 11 one night he was at his parents' house when he got a call from Travis with instructions to meet him at a gas station. Belman went, wondering what would come out of the meeting. When they met, Travis told him they were going to go to LeBron's house nearby and show him the movie. Did LeBron know they were coming? No, Travis said. Belman was petrified. They were going to show up unannounced at midnight? They did, and LeBron welcomed them. When he watched the clip,

LeBron was both emotional and excited. He watched it several times over. He'd been transported back to high school days. He was only twenty-three, but he was enjoying the nostalgia.

A few days later LeBron went to Los Angeles, where he was set to co-host the annual ESPY Awards, a sports award show put on every year during the Major League Baseball All-Star break by ESPN. His co-host was Jimmy Kimmel, who was the host of a late-night show on ESPN's sister network, ABC. ABC also had the contract to air NBA games including the NBA Finals, which LeBron had just played in for the first time. Synergy all around.

As he was working alongside Kimmel to prepare for the show, LeBron showed Kimmel the DVD in a dressing room. Kimmel loved it and recommended to LeBron what he'd already been thinking: that he turn it into a full-scale documentary. Shortly thereafter, Belman got a call from Maverick Carter. They wanted to partner with Belman on making it a complete film. Naturally, Belman had an important question: Would they let him direct it? The answer was yes. Holding the footage and not selling it was about to pay off. By this point, two years into their experiment with LRMR, LeBron and Carter were very focused on making partnership deals where they had partial control and partial ownership in projects. That is exactly what Belman was hoping to get.

"I'll never forget when they called," Belman said. "I got the sense they wanted a seat at the table but also that they wanted to do whatever they could to make it a success."

None of them knew it yet, but this was a major step that would end up contributing to changing the course of the way LeBron went about his business career. With Carter and LeBron set to be executive producers, to get the project started they had to form a production company. After some consideration they decided to call it SpringHill Productions. SpringHill was the name of the housing project where LeBron moved with his mother when they were finally able to get a stable home. He lived there happily in a mid-rise building during his high school years. There was no way to know this then, because they were focused on building LRMR, the marketing company, but SpringHill Productions would end up being an extremely important operation to them.

With LeBron and his former teammates willing to take part in additional interviews and provide more content in return for the film, the documentary that had collected dust for years quickly took shape. They made a deal with producer Harvey Mason Jr., who was equally impressed with the reel and had helped make the movie *Dreamgirls* and specialized in making movies that featured music. Years later he'd be one of the producers of the animated musical *Sing*.

Music artists who had a relationship with LeBron, such as Jay-Z and Drake, agreed to contribute to the soundtrack, which was going to be a major part of the project. Then there was an idea for a book. A few years earlier a movie came out about the storied 1966 Texas Western basketball team and their coach, Don Haskins. At the same time as the movie, Haskins released a compatible autobiography. It wasn't an original concept, but it had worked for the basketball audience.

LeBron had read and liked the book *Friday Night Lights*, which was about a high school football team in Texas that had been made into a movie and a TV series. LRMR contacted and then hired the author, Buzz Bissinger, to co-write LeBron and his friends' high school story, which would be published alongside Belman's documentary.

This opportunity came at a heady time for the LRMR group. While their athlete representation arm had yet to take off, they were trying to expand the horizons of the client they did have: LeBron. About that same time, they'd hired a research firm to do a deep dive into what the market thought of LeBron, specifically how well known he was. The results showed there was good awareness about him among hardcore basketball fans—he could hardly be missed when watching just about any NBA game. Even if he wasn't playing in it, there was a good chance there'd be a commercial with him on it during one of the breaks. But his popularity among casual NBA fans and regular consumers wasn't as strong.

"Many people who bought his shoes were fans of LeBron," said Matt Powell, a sports apparel industry analyst for the NPD Group. "He struggled to break out and cross over to casual fans."

As part of his Nike deal from years earlier, LeBron agreed to go on a promotional trip to China every summer. China was a blossoming market for basketball, and on volume alone the country was important to the shoe manufacturers like Nike. By the mid-2000s there was a growing focus on the coming 2008 Olympics in Beijing. The attention of the world and, perhaps more important for someone selling shoes, the focus of all of China was going to be on the star athletes like him. With his remarkable 2006–07 season, during which he played in his first Finals, Carter and LeBron sensed he was on the cusp of taking a leap in popularity. They hoped to find and develop new marketing opportunities, and eventually dollars, that could come with it.

One of the first moves was to hire a New York–based publicist, Keith Estabrook, who came recommended to LeBron and his group by Jay-Z and Steve Stoute. Estabrook had connections in the literary and fashion worlds, areas where Carter and LeBron wanted to expand the LeBron brand.

Hosting the ESPYs—where LeBron opened the show with a singing and dancing ode to Bobby Brown and his classic hit "My Prerogative"—was only part of the rollout. LeBron also hosted the 2007 premiere of *Saturday Night Live*, where he performed a basketball skit with cast member Bill Hader. They didn't know it at the time, but they would end up doing a movie together years later.

LeBron also agreed to do a full feature with *60 Minutes*. He charmed reporter Steve Kroft: At one point during the interview in the gym at his high school, he playfully tossed a shot from beyond half court and swished it. Kroft, a hard-nosed legend, was flabbergasted, literally doing a pirouette as LeBron joked: "I'm one take, baby." CBS used it in promos for the interview the week it ran.

As a part of this process, LRMR had started putting together an annual event they called the LeBron Summit, where executives who worked with him in his various endorsement deals were brought together for two days of meetings to attempt corporate brainstorming. It was an unusual event and certainly not something athletes typically hosted. But to Carter's credit, it was innovative, and LeBron had the juice to draw the executives from Nike, Coca-Cola, Upper Deck, Cadbury Schweppes, Cub Cadet, and Microsoft to Akron in the middle of the summer to take part. In 2007, Duke coach Mike Krzyzewski, who had gotten to know LeBron the previous summer as the head coach of Team USA, was the speaker at the opening dinner. Estabrook had arranged for a reporter from *Fortune* magazine to be there to chronicle it.

Over an eighteen-month period leading up to the Beijing Olympics, LeBron would appear on the covers of *Fortune*, *Men's Health*, *GQ*, and *Vogue* as the plan to amplify his fame rolled onward. Reporters interviewed LeBron as he flew on private jets. Reporters interviewed him on the set of commercial shoots. And so on. In one profile in *Advertising Age*, the writer posited that LRMR had the goal of making LeBron a "global icon" by the time the 2008 Olympics were over. It seemed rather ambitious, especially with the group still fighting the perception that they were out of their depth. But their game plan was their game plan, and they were going all out to execute it.

The story the non-sports reporters often wanted was about how LeBron was working with his friends in business ventures. It was an unusual narrative for a star athlete, and it added depth, which is what publications were looking for. LeBron and Carter had plenty of experience dealing with media, and the access had been well designed to coincide with projects the young entrepreneurs were trying to publicize. As each feature was published and photos of LeBron in suits started to become routine, the rough edges were smoothed. Carter became more well known, especially to readers in the financial world, where he was looking to establish more legitimacy.

The only significant misstep during that time wasn't really LeBron or Carter's fault. The *Vogue* cover, in the spring of 2008, was hailed as a breakthrough when it was announced. It was supposed to be because LeBron was to be the first African American man ever to be on the cover of the fashion bible. It was given top billing in every way as famed photographer Annie Leibovitz came in to do the photo shoot with him and world-famous model Gisele Bündchen. Leibovitz, who later came back to Akron to shoot LeBron for a *Vanity Fair* spread, enjoyed working with him and had lobbied *Vogue* editor Anna Wintour to choose LeBron for the cover from the array of athletes and models photographed together in the magazine. But when the issue hit shelves, it ended up becoming somewhat infamous.

In the shot that made the cover, a mouth-agape LeBron is wearing a black tank top and shorts and dribbling a ball with one hand while the other is draped around the slim waist of Bündchen, who is flinging her hair back in a sleek green gown. Critics—and there were many—felt the scene mimicked age-old photos of King Kong grasping the blond-haired Fay Wray. It was deemed insensitive by some and downright racist by others. Personally, I was confused as to why fashion-conscious LeBron would waste his grand moment on the cover of a world-renowned fashion magazine by appearing in basketball practice gear. The idea, apparently, was to show a contrast of the great athlete and the glamorous model, each in their element, which for Le-Bron was athletic wear and for Bündchen was couture. Another shot ran inside the magazine of LeBron and Giselle twisting around each other in an elegant and striking pose. Had that run on the cover, it probably would have gotten a completely different reception. This was a photo more befitting of Leibovitz's talent, in my opinion, which didn't matter. But if visibility was what LeBron and his group wanted, the *Vogue* cover absolutely got them that.

Meanwhile, after all the years of waiting and working, Belman finished his documentary. They decided to call it *More than a Game*, an ode to the storyline that while it focused on basketball and LeBron, it was also about the friendships and struggles of the five teenagers. LeBron's role in the movie was roughly equal to the others, an aspect of the film that got LeBron invested in the project. Obviously, he was to be the star, but like the way he preferred to play, he wanted to share the ball, so to speak. Belman, who had been there to see it, agreed. That construction may not have happened had a larger operation been in control and wanted to make the film more LeBron-centric for commercial reasons. From a documentary perspective, though, the movie was attractive because of the raw footage of the players in their element and the open interviews that went along with it.

The project got a major boost when the Toronto

International Film Festival, one of the most influential festivals in the world, agreed to accept the movie and show it on opening weekend. In early September 2008, the group flew to Toronto for the screening. It was packed. It had taken more than five years of work to get the project to this point. And it was a complete hit.

The crowd gave it a standing ovation, with media outlets reporting that it lasted several minutes. As he soaked in the applause, tears welled in LeBron's eyes. "This is the first time I've cried, in basketball or anything, since we lost that national championship game in eighth grade," LeBron said after he left the screening. "This is authentic."

The People's Choice Award, the highest honor at the festival, went to *Slumdog Millionaire*, which won the Academy Award for Best Picture a few months later. The first runner-up was *More than a Game*. Some of the People's Choice Award winners over the years in Toronto included *Chariots of Fire*, *The Princess Bride*, *Shine*, *American Beauty*, *The King's Speech*, *Silver Linings Playbook*, and *12 Years a Slave*.

Getting first runner-up was a very big deal; it was a victory in itself. It was an emotional moment for all of them because it was their story, but there was now a real interest in the film. Immediately, distributors wanted to meet to discuss buying the rights to the movie. It became clear it would be released in theaters.

"Maverick had this gleaming look in his eyes,"

Belman remembered. "He knew that this was going to take them to the next level."

He was right. This may not have been part of their plan when they sat in Carter's mother's kitchen and plotted their marketing firm. This wasn't on their course when they were hoping to use 2008 to catapult LeBron into a global icon. But here they were. LeBron was about to get into the media business in a big way.

Chapter 7

# THE DEALMAKER

For a time, LeBron James was the fastest player in the NBA with the ball from end to end. His long strides and fast-twitch muscles enabled him to cover ground with amazing efficiency. But you should have seen him move through an airport.

It wasn't unusual for LeBron to fly commercial in his early days as a pro. He flew private on certain business matters and when he flew with the Cavs on road trips. But it wasn't all the time. When he had to do so he had a practice of speed-walking through the terminal, usually with his head down and a hoodie on. By the time people noticed who he was, he was already gone, which was the point.

It was moving on from this inconvenience of fame that brought LeBron in contact with Jesse Itzler.

Itzler and his partner had founded a company called

Marquis Jet, which sold private jet time in blocks of hours, a product that was attractive for pro athletes and celebrities who wanted to fly private but didn't need to own their own plane even as a fractional owner. Itzler, who became wealthy as an entrepreneur in various businesses during his career, made it a priority to personally and aggressively market the company by forging relationships with customers and potential customers.

Once he got on a commercial flight from New York to Los Angeles because he learned young stars Ben Affleck and Matt Damon were going to be guests on one of Marquis Jet's planes. He made it to L.A. in time to get on the private plane and personally pitch them on the service. In another move to appeal to Hollywood elite, he gave away free flights to the producers of *Entourage* in return for getting product placement in the show because he knew how influential it was within Hollywood.

Part of this campaign was to market to NBA players, and Itzler recruited them using nontraditional methods. For example, the company bought a sponsorship within the visiting locker room at New Jersey Nets and New Jersey Devils games. These were ads meant to appeal only to the few dozen visiting millionaire athletes that came through each week. Itzler had been an NBA fan in New York for years. He briefly had a singing career where his biggest hit was making the catchy "Go NY Go," which became the Knicks anthem in the 1990s. He later bought a piece of the Atlanta Hawks with his wife, a fellow entrepreneur who had founded Spanx.

When LeBron looked to leave commercial travel behind him, part of it was through Itzler and Marquis Jet. It ended up being an important relationship beyond that initial transaction. Itzler, LeBron, and Maverick Carter later formed a company together selling energy strips that dissolved on the tongue. But the most important thing Itzler and his partner Kenny Dichter did was introduce Carter and LeBron to Paul Wachter.

It is fair to say that Wachter has been the single most influential force in LeBron's business portfolio, even though he's typically very much in the background. With Wachter as the dealmaker and the guide, LeBron has forged partnerships and created companies that have added hundreds of millions to his net worth. Wachter introduced LeBron and Carter to aspects of the entertainment world and helped show them how to create wealth from their best resource: their popularity. Just about every major move LeBron has made in the business world since 2005 has had at least some of Wachter's fingerprints on it. Some of them have been a Wachter production from start to finish. It's been one of the most rewarding relationships of LeBron's career.

LeBron has made it clear that his decision to choose Nike over the bigger offer from Reebok was the best business decision of his life. Choosing Wachter as a partner may be up there with it. It was a shrewd and unconventional choice that came after plenty of vetting. But Carter and LeBron, who were in their twenties, did their research and picked Wachter, a man in his mid-fifties who had almost nothing to do with the sports business during his career. And it was a brilliant choice.

Wachter's background is straight East Coast blue blood; his résumé is absolutely sparkling. He has an MBA from Wharton and a law degree from Columbia. He clerked for a judge on the Court of Appeals. He worked as a tax attorney at the New York powerhouse firm Paul, Weiss, Rifkind, Wharton and Garrison. He spent time with Bear Stearns and other New York firms as an investment banker. The list goes on and on. He's on impressive boards of directors and part of wonderful charities.

Where Wachter's career story takes a unique turn was a relationship he started back in 1981. When he was working as a clerk for the Court of Appeals, he became friends with another clerk, Bobby Shriver, son of Sargent Shriver and Eunice Kennedy Shriver. Wachter then met Bobby's sister, a young television journalist named Maria, and her boyfriend, a bodybuilder with good looks, an Austrian accent, and Hollywood aspirations named Arnold Schwarzenegger.

Schwarzenegger and Wachter connected, and not

just over movies. Schwarzenegger was interested in bodybuilding and the entertainment industry but also in business, especially real estate. With some of the money he made from winning bodybuilding competitions like Mr. Universe, he started buying apartment and retail buildings in Santa Monica in the late 1970s. By the time he became a household name when he got his big break as an actor in *Conan the Barbarian* in 1982, he was already a millionaire through these investments.

The relationship developed, and Wachter took on Schwarzenegger as a client. In 1997, Schwarzenegger convinced Wachter to leave his job after more than twenty years in the business and come work full-time with him. It was then that Wachter founded Main Street Advisors in Santa Monica in an office just outside Schwarzenegger's. The first major deal Wachter did for Schwarzenegger was buying a 747 jet from Singapore Airlines and then leasing it back to the airline, an unusual yet creative investment that has characterized Schwarzenegger and Wachter's work together. When Schwarzenegger ran for governor of California in 2003, Wachter took over the blind trusts to care for his assets as well as those of Arnold's wife at the time, Maria Shriver.

One of the early investments that Wachter made with Schwarzenegger was in Planet Hollywood, the movie-themed restaurant chain that later became a casino in Las Vegas. Ultimately, Planet Hollywood filed for Chapter 11. But it was the concept that was relevant. Schwarzenegger, as well as other celebrities, were given equity in the business for lending their name, making promotional appearances, and providing some memorabilia.

Finding an apartment building in an area that was about to increase in value is hard and risky. Owning a jumbo jet based on the other side of the world is complicated and risky. Getting equity in a business in exchange for something in ready supply—a person's fame—was a much more tantalizing proposition. That is what the Planet Hollywood deal was for Schwarzenegger, and it became an instructive way of doing business for Wachter.

By the time LeBron agreed to have Wachter make business deals for him, Wachter had a small but noteworthy list of clients. They included the musician Bono from the group U2, legendary music producer Jimmy Iovine, and Tom Werner, the television producer who had made hit shows like *Roseanne* and *The Cosby Show*. What was just as important as these names was the length of time they'd been with Wachter.

He purposely had a small client list because he wanted long and strong relationships. This was how LeBron preferred to work, too. It was part of his thinking when choosing Nike and Coca-Cola when he started out. It was one of the reasons he'd put his trust in Carter. LeBron wanted to form a bond that would last. Even though Wachter was very different from him, they saw in his background and through conversations that he was a careful and thoughtful investor. He was the kind of person they ultimately wanted to be in business with.

One of the things Wachter did for LeBron in their early years together was help arrange an introduction to Warren Buffett, the world-famous investor. Wachter had done business with Berkshire Hathaway, Buffett's firm. LeBron was interested in meeting with the so-called Oracle of Omaha. Wachter knew Buffett liked to be around sports stars. Buffett had developed a relationship with baseball star Alex Rodriguez and football star Ndamukong Suh. It was arranged for LeBron to travel to Omaha and meet with Buffett. They filmed a little segment together that Buffett used at his company's annual meeting, with Buffett allegedly beating LeBron in a game of one-on-one. They ate cheeseburgers, had milkshakes, and talked investment strategy. LeBron was happy, Buffett was happy, and Wachter had helped make it happen.

LeBron is "very clever in the way he looks at his business off the court," Buffett told me in 2009 when he attended a Cavs game in Cleveland. "He has the right priorities. I wish I was as smart about business when I was his age."

Wachter taking advantage of a partner or a connection to open a door to LeBron to leverage his fame and influence was a process that would repeat itself over and over. It resulted in myriad business deals that made LeBron lots of money. Sometimes ideas from Carter or LeBron would be the impetus; sometimes it would be Wachter. But it really started working. It was much more successful and profitable than trying to chase down athletes to represent and earn a commission on, like LRMR had been trying. At its core, it wasn't all that different from the concept LeBron's friends had when they were starting out and they pocketed a few thousand from parties where people would pay a couple hundred bucks to get some access. Wachter elevated that to the billionaire level, a stratosphere that was more fitting of LeBron's stature and sensibility. And LeBron and Carter quickly learned that finding partnerships was much more fulfilling than simply taking a check for doing an endorsement.

This concept fit with what LeBron wanted when he left agent Aaron Goodwin and went out on his own. He had wanted more control over what was happening with his business. And it fit with what Wachter had learned in his years in the business: the importance of getting equity and the pathways that celebrity could create.

The first major business deal Wachter put LeBron into was, believe it or not, bicycles. During the summers when he was off from the NBA, LeBron liked to stay in shape by riding his bicycle. His home in Akron was near a nature reserve that ran along the winding

Cuyahoga River and had hundreds of miles of trails. Some days he would go out with Randy Mims and ride for miles and miles. In enabled him to get a workout without pounding on his legs.

As they discussed going into business together, Carter and LeBron felt it was important to choose investments that were authentic to him. He didn't want to sell something he didn't believe in; making those types of moves could cause problems down the line. And he didn't really want to invest in something he didn't believe in, either. Cycling was something he believed in. LeBron had set up a foundation and wanted it aimed at helping children in his hometown. One of the first major events it organized was an annual bikeathon, where children would help raise money by biking with LeBron and other celebrities across the city. As part of the event, the foundation would donate bikes to kids who didn't have them so they could stay active.

Carter wondered if LeBron could become a partner with Schwinn, a large bicycle maker. But at the same time Wachter was connected with a private equity company called Pegasus Capital Advisors. One of its holdings was a bicycle company called Cannondale, a once high-end manufacturer from Connecticut that had fallen on hard times; Pegasus bought it in bankruptcy in 2003. By 2007, the company had started a turnaround and looked like it might be headed for a sale.

Using his connections, Wachter arranged for LeBron

to be able to buy into the company with Carter also getting a small stake. But the investment didn't come until after LeBron had researched the company and felt an affinity for its product. The investment made national news and increased brand awareness, exactly the type of positive impact that taking on an investor of LeBron's profile was designed to do for Cannondale and Pegasus. Carter advised the company on some marketing campaigns. And it didn't feel awkward— LeBron was known to be into riding bikes, so buying in made sense. It was a smart if unexpected marriage. Maybe not as exotic as buying a 747, but more financially sound.

A year later Cannondale was sold to a Canadian conglomerate. Pegasus reportedly nearly quadrupled its investment. Carter made six figures on his investment. LeBron made seven figures. Wachter got his cut and once again made everyone happy. A trade publication, *Buyouts* magazine, named Pegasus's deal with Cannondale the "Turnaround of the Year." The company sent Carter a trophy to celebrate the achievement.

The reward of turning around the Cannondale investment was intoxicating. LeBron had done much bigger deals. Through a new contract he'd signed with the Cavs that agent Leon Rose put together in 2006, LeBron made several million a month in salary during the basketball season. But their plan to get involved with something they were truly interested in had paid

Agent Aaron Goodwin (*left*) made huge deals for LeBron with Nike and Coca-Cola. Here they are in 2003, just before a commercial shoot for Nike at the Forum in Los Angeles. (*Photo by Steve Grayson/ WireImage*)

LeBron and Maverick Carter have known each other since they were children. Their relationship is based on trust, loyalty, and the desire to maximize opportunity. They've failed together and succeeded together. Here they are at the 2016 All-Star Weekend in Toronto. (*Photo by George Pimentel/WireImage*)

The Four Horsemen, as LeBron's close friends call themselves, show their loyalty with hand signals when posing for photos. Only a few people have been allowed into the inner circle. One of them, Wes Wesley (*behind and to the left of LeBron*), introduced LeBron to rap artist Jay-Z. Here Carter, Rich Paul, Wesley, LeBron, and Jay-Z celebrate the opening of Jay-Z's 40/40 club in Las Vegas in 2007. (*Photo by Johnny Nunez/WireImage*)

Paul Wachter (*right, with Maverick Carter*) has been a supreme dealmaker and relationship creator for LeBron for more than a decade. He and Carter have put together deals totaling hundreds of millions for LeBron. (*Photo by Allen Berezovsky/WireImage*)

LeBron has maintained a relationship with world-famous investor Warren Buffett since 2006. Buffett has attended several games to support his friend, including this one in Cleveland in 2014. (*Photo by David Liam Kyle/NBAE via Getty Images*)

Jimmy Iovine (*left*) and LeBron have been strong partners for years. Here they are celebrating one of their first projects together, the launch of the soundtrack from the documentary *More than a Game* in 2009, with Mary J. Blige, who contributed to the album. (*Photo by Johnny Nunez/WireImage*)

The 2008 Olympics were a vital marketing opportunity for LeBron and his partners. His role in leading the "Redeem Team" to gold was a career highlight and helped build his brand in China. (*Photo by Jesse D. Garrabrant/NBAE via Getty Images*)

The idea to give Beats to LeBron's Olympic teammates in Beijing was a transcendent plan. The players wore them all over the city, which helped launch the company and made these oversized headphones a fashionable must-have—all for nearly no cost. (*Photo by Jesse D. Garrabrant/NBAE via Getty Images*)

*The Decision* in 2010 was the brainchild of famed sports broadcaster Jim Gray, who approached Carter with the plan. This is moments before the show in Greenwich, Connecticut, as Gray goes over some of the scripted questions leading up to LeBron's announcement of where he was taking his talents. (*Photo by Larry Busacca/Getty Images for Estabrook Group*)

LeBron's first game back in Cleveland on December 2, 2010, was one of the most stressful moments of his life. But he's always been more comfortable with Carter courtside, and LeBron needed him on this night. (*Photo by Gregory Shamus/Getty Images*)

In 2011, LeBron made a revolutionary deal with Fenway Sports Group that enabled him to become a minority owner in English soccer power Liverpool FC. He visited the club's historic stadium, Anfield, for a match that fall. (*Photo by Andrew Powell/Liverpool FC via Getty Images*)

Promoting his brand overseas has been a focus of LeBron and his partners since he was a teenager. Here he's showing off his skills at an event in London for Nike in 2011. (*Photo by Dean Mouhtaropoulos/ Getty Images for Nike*)

LeBron's Nike contract calls for him to make annual trips to China. He's traveled across the country over the years doing camps, meeting fans, and posing for photos as he's become more famous. This is in 2017 in Beijing, as thousands of fans get into a selfie outside a Nike store. (*Photo by VCG/VCG via Getty Images*)

LeBron and Chris Paul have been great friends for years. Here they finish LeBron's bike-a-thon in his hometown of Akron, Ohio, in 2009. These events were the beginning of a foundation that would change the lives of thousands of children. (*Photo by David Liam Kyle/NBAE via Getty Images*)

Part of the reason for LeBron's move to L.A. in 2018 was to be closer to the entertainment business. Maverick Carter and Jimmy Iovine, seen here sharing a conversation at one of his first Laker games, have big plans for their content businesses in the future. (*Photo by Allen Berezovsky/Getty Images*)

off. And it came from the money man they'd selected to find these deals for them. This was what LeBron and Carter wanted to replicate and add zeros to.

As they looked to expand to more of these ventures, that authenticity principle became one of the most important elements of deals Carter sought out for LeBron. If it didn't pass that initial test, it was a no go. Carter told me that he was routinely offered seven-figure deals that weren't worth taking to LeBron because it didn't meet this standard. Sometimes he'd tell LeBron about a call that came with an offer, and LeBron would just ignore it and ask Carter about a vintage of wine he'd just tried. And if a product was borderline authentic, steps were taken to make sure consumers could be convinced.

In 2014, for example, Carter noticed that Kia had launched a luxury model that retailed for more than $60,000, a big departure for the company. Kia had been a primary NBA sponsor for nearly a decade, and LeBron had won and given away four of them to charity when he won Most Valuable Player Awards in 2009, 2010, 2012, and 2013. Los Angeles Clippers star Blake Griffin was the face of the Korean carmaker in the United States, making a series of clever and self-deprecating ads to sell their middle-market sedan, the Optima. In 2011, he'd hit marketing gold when he jumped over an Optima in his final maneuver and won the Slam Dunk Contest. Griffin is whimsical and has a dry sense of humor, and the ads worked.

This new Kia model, the K900, sounded and looked more like a BMW. At least that's what the company was trying to sell. Carter believed it was a car LeBron could sell. LeBron had never done ads for a major car manufacturer before; having a millionaire athlete sell anything less than a luxury brand seems hollow. Tiger Woods pitched Buicks for years, and so did Shaquille O'Neal, but it wasn't the perfect fit.

Griffin was an outlier in this regard. Carter had contacts with Kia through the NBA and got one of the cars for LeBron to test drive. When LeBron liked it, he and Carter went back to the company looking to do a marketing deal.

To help keep the concept on brand, LeBron used social media accounts to show himself using the car even before the deal was announced. Kia made a commercial with LeBron answering people on social media who doubted he actually drove a Kia, even a high-end one. They even made a deal with TNT to show LeBron arriving at a game the network was broadcasting in the K900. Not everyone believed it. LeBron did like to drive his Ferraris and Lamborghinis. For most games he was driven in a specially outfitted Mercedes van. But he did like the Kia, and it was important for the deal that he make that as authentic as possible.

This sort of thinking and partnership building helped Wachter create an important connection. In 2008, Wachter connected LeBron to one of his valued

personal clients: Jimmy Iovine. Iovine was a legend in
the music industry. He had an almost uncanny ability
to meet and ingratiate himself with stars and then
deliver high-level results. He got his foot in the door
by working with John Lennon, infuriating his family
by going to work with him at the studio on Easter
Sunday. He produced Bruce Springsteen's legendary
*Born to Run* album after months of exhaustive editing.
He talked Springsteen into giving Patti Smith the song
"Because the Night," creating an unexpected smash hit.
He made Tom Petty and the Heartbreakers millions
with their classic album *Damn the Torpedoes*. He dated
Stevie Nicks. He founded Interscope Records. And a
lot more.

In 2006, with the record industry derailed by
streaming music websites, Iovine and longtime business partner Andre Young, better known as the rapper
Dr. Dre, began discussing other ways to make money
as record sales were drying up. At first, Dr. Dre wanted
to try to create a shoe line. Iovine waved him off and
said they should make something they know: music
speakers. They started a long design and testing phase.
By 2008, the speaker idea had been reworked, and Dr.
Dre and Iovine had developed oversized headphones
that they believed delivered superior sound quality.
They were called Beats by Dre. One of the people
who helped them along the way, including making a
deal with an Australian company to manufacture the

headphones, was Iovine's valued business connection: Wachter.

These headphones looked like they might be a hard sell. They had Dr. Dre's name on them, but they were huge, covering the ears like a professional sound mixer would use. It wasn't the style at the time. And they were expensive, as much as $400, an entirely new price level for a market that was used to headphones that came with iPhones for free or, even at the high end, around $100. Iovine had always been a marketing genius. He was as gifted at packaging as he was at producing. Beats didn't have much of a marketing budget, and they couldn't put ads on television or in major magazines to announce their product to the market.

Wachter had an idea, though. He had an influencer for a business partner, someone who could help make oversize and expensive headphones cool, just like he could make $200 pairs of signature Nikes cool. But Wachter knew that it wasn't as simple as recruiting LeBron and getting him to wear the headphones. Maybe it would have worked years earlier, when LeBron just wanted a check, but now those deals didn't move the needle. The partnership first had to grow in the other direction.

At the time, LeBron and Carter's production business, SpringHill, was getting started as they were involved in putting out *More than a Game*. Wachter put Iovine and LeBron together on the documentary. Iovine became an investor in the film and got an executive producer title. It added credibility to the project and deepened the relationship. Iovine also took advantage of the situation by hosting screenings for the movie at his home. He always had a pair or two of the headphones to show off to the stream of influencers who came to see the show. And being part of the movie put him directly in business with LeBron and Carter as they headed toward the Toronto Film Festival.

Iovine had showed Carter and LeBron the Beats headphones, too. Carter and LeBron had promised they would be authentic, and they liked them. It was something they could see themselves using. Of course, it helped that they had Dr. Dre's name on them. LeBron had grown up listening to Dr. Dre's solo work and his iconic group, NWA. They could see these headphones selling. They could see these headphones on NBA players' ears.

It was then that Carter and Iovine came up with a plan. Carter told Iovine about the rise of a new economy, in which players had become fashion plates when they arrived and departed venues. Arena loading docks had become red carpets, a place where trends were born. Carter asked for a dozen pairs of the headphones. The idea was for LeBron to give them away as gifts to his teammates on Team USA when he went to play in the Beijing Olympics that summer. It was a great gift idea: The players had a twelve-hour flight to

China plus lots of time on buses as they sat in traffic around the capital. LeBron was one of the biggest stars in the world. He was using this cutting-edge electronic equipment no one else had, so why wouldn't his teammates? It was a cool and smart concept. In practice, it turned out to be brilliant.

As players arrived at the arena for games, when they left practice gyms, and when they did interviews as millions watched around the globe, they wore brand-new Beats headphones around their head or around their necks. They were big, bright, and different looking, with a unique logo. No one had seen them before. With all these basketball stars showing them off, they became an item of intrigue, an item that was desired.

Beats hadn't paid millions to the International Olympic Committee to be a sponsor like Nike and Coca-Cola. They didn't buy expensive television ads during the games. They didn't pay the athletes millions for their endorsement. Yet all the players had become de facto walking billboards for the company and thanked LeBron for being so kind as to hook them up.

Leading up to the games, Coke had spent heavily on a campaign with Yao Ming and LeBron, flying them to a warehouse in Cleveland over the previous All-Star Weekend to make an ad. It was the only time in his life LeBron had to stand on a riser—he couldn't get into the same frame as the 7-foot-6 Yao without it. That was cool, too. But what Beats did with next to nothing was more influential. From Iovine's perspective, he'd taken a connection to Carter and LeBron through Wachter and made a small investment in a documentary to strengthen a relationship that led to a marketing grand slam. Again, it was Carter with the concept, LeBron with the execution, and Wachter connecting partners and making everyone happy.

Wachter, who became a Beats board of directors member, later helped put together a deal that made LeBron a partner in Beats. He agreed to promote the company but also got a small percentage of ownership. The gifting of the headphones to other influencers became a core marketing strategy for the company. LeBron gave out customized versions to his Cleveland Cavaliers teammates and then his All-Star teammates the following season. Years later, at the 2012 Olympics in London, Beats doubled down. They rented out a building and created an "athletes only" clubhouse and encouraged athletes from all nations to come and spend time there, even going so far as to hint it was a private place to have dates with fellow athletes. When they came, they were given Beats headphones in their country's colors. They all left as walking billboards, too. It was another brilliant strategy to co-opt willing athletes.

Over the next six years, LeBron continued to market Beats. The brand eventually moved into television ads, and LeBron was featured in the first commercial, shot inside a hotel gymnasium in downtown Miami. He specifically was marketing a smaller earbud-style version that was useful to basketball players when practicing.

"One of the things LeBron taught us was the degree that audio affected performance," Luke Wood, the president of Beats, explained. "It gives athletes a refuge when they need it, inspiration when they need it, and helps them with preparation. LeBron didn't just help us market the product, he helped us develop it. And because he was wearing them and he's one of the highest-profile athletes in the world, the product became a conversation piece."

By the early 2010s, Beats were ubiquitous. LeBron had so many different specialized pairs he wore that they became as much a part of his ensemble as his Nikes. At the height of popularity in early 2014, Beats agreed to sell itself to Apple for a whopping $3 billion in cash, a number that stunned both the industry and Wall Street. By then the company was selling speakers and had developed its own subscription music service, which was ironic because it was those types of services that had driven Iovine and Dr. Dre into this enterprise in the first place.

Beats had taken on investors and financing over the years as it grew. *Forbes* reported that Dr. Dre owned about 25 percent of the company at the sale. It was the greatest business deal of their lifetimes, earning them hundreds of millions each. Getting in on the ground floor and helping the company launch paid off hugely for LeBron as well.

When the sale closed, LeBron got a check for more than $50 million, making Beats the second biggest business deal of his career after Nike. He also retained a deal with the company after the sale to continue to promote the brand, which also got him into a relationship with Apple.

This was the sort of outcome he and Carter had dreamed of when they got into marketing and investing. Yes, the product had benefited simply from being attached to LeBron. There were other influencers in other fields, particularly music, that had fueled its growth as well. Iovine's relentless selling to his web of famous friends was a vital aspect. Wachter had made a couple of complex legal maneuvers to help get Beats stronger control of the company—one of the company's former partners sued Dr. Dre, Iovine, and Wachter for being deceptive, but a judge threw it out— and had played a key role in making the sale happen. Everybody got paid handsomely.

All of LeBron's core group had played important roles. Wachter was already a valued member of LeBron's operation, but this one bonded him for life. It was all about personal relationships, long-term thinking, and leveraging value.

Within months of the sale, Dr. Dre paid $40 million

to buy Tom Brady and Gisele Bündchen's mansion in Brentwood outside Los Angeles. Soon after, LeBron spent $21 million on his own mansion in Los Angeles.

But that was all about a much bigger deal down the line.

# Chapter 8

# SUMMER CAMP FOR BILLIONAIRES

The cottages that line Old Dollar Road in Sun Valley, Idaho, are both quaint and luxurious, their decks overlooking the mountains of Sawtooth National Forest, a lake stocked with paddle boats, or the fairways of the Robert Trent Jones–designed golf course. They rent for up to $3,500 per night.

During the second week of July, when summer is in full bloom in central Idaho, the private jets start arriving by the hundreds at Friedman Memorial Airport. Flowers line the back patio at the Grill at Knob Hill as plates of perfectly cooked filet mignon and fresh trout pour out of the kitchen every evening. Nondisclosure agreements are in place, so no one will talk about how bad the karaoke is on the roped-off second floor of Whiskey Jacques'. Luxury SUVs with tinted glass line Highway 75.

Since 1983, the Allen & Company media conference has developed into the so-called "summer camp for billionaires," a four-day invitation-only event that has become a place for brainstorming, deal making, and elbow rubbing for media moguls. Legend has it the AOL and Time Warner merger was hatched in Sun Valley. Jeff Bezos, the founder of Amazon, started talks to buy the *Washington Post* from the Graham family there. And many more.

At the conference in 2009 the usual faces were in attendance: Bill Gates, Warren Buffett, Mark Zuckerberg, Sumner Redstone, and so on. But a new face stood out among the crowd, someone none of the moguls had ever expected to see at this event: LeBron James, who was coming to attend panels and exclusive Q&As and learn what it's like to be a media executive.

Several years earlier Maverick Carter caught a ride on one of Cavs owner Dan Gilbert's jets on a flight from New York to Cleveland ahead of the opening game of the season. Also on the jet was Steve Greenberg, one of Allen & Company's executives. Allen & Company had assisted Gilbert in his purchase of the Cavs in 2005, and Gilbert was a valued client. When they were introduced, Carter asked Greenberg how he and LeBron could get an invitation to attend the conference. It stunned Greenberg that Carter had ever even heard of the gathering. It had been a struggle at times for Carter to get credibility as an agent as he fought the perception that he was an ancillary hanger-on in LeBron's universe. Selling himself as someone interested in getting into the media business was a taller order.

Carter did it an inch at a time, making it his business to do research and become well versed so that when he had opportunities, like he did with Greenberg, he could create and extend relationships. Gilbert, who was a regular in Sun Valley every July, had encouraged LeBron to attend the conference in the past, but LeBron's schedule with Team USA made it hard. Between 2006 and 2008, LeBron had committed a significant portion of every summer to the national team. But in 2009 there was a hole in the schedule.

By the summer of 2009, Carter and LeBron had been through an invigorating process surrounding *More than a Game*, their documentary with director Kristopher Belman, which had educated them on the media business and, frankly, got them more committed to get in deeper. They had started working with a new partner, Hollywood powerhouse agency William Morris Endeavor, to get the movie sold to a distributor. LeBron had leaned on his trusted sponsors, Nike and Coca-Cola, who had pledged to back the movie with some marketing dollars as they looked to land a deal that would get the documentary into theaters. After the buzz was created in Toronto, a small bidding war developed, and the new media executives leaned on Jimmy Iovine, their new partner in Beats, among others, to help close the deal. In all, they met with seven distribution companies who were interested in buying the rights.

"Maverick was in all of the pitch meetings but he deferred to Jimmy and let him handle the process," Belman said. "And wherever Jimmy was, his partner Paul Wachter was with him. That was how they did business."

With Carter watching and learning, the group ended up getting a multimillion-dollar package from Lionsgate. As Carter had predicted, it had taken them to a whole new level. They were in meetings with studio executives now. They were working with Iovine's label, Interscope, on a major soundtrack.

When Carter and LeBron put together the annual summer trip to China for Nike and Coke business, they turned it into an international tour to publicize the film, which would also be released overseas. It turned into an international bonanza with LeBron doing not only events that promoted his partners but those that would spread awareness of the movie.

The first stop was in Silver Spring, Maryland, where the film made its US debut at a documentary film festival. It was part of a memorable day. Before going to the Washington, DC, suburb, LeBron was a guest of President Barack Obama at the White House with Carter, Rich Paul, and Randy Mims. The four friends, mocked a few years earlier for their inexperience and lack of direction, posed for photos in the Oval Office. LeBron had campaigned for Obama in the battleground state of Ohio, which Obama had carried the previous fall. To the victor go the spoils and the White House invites.

There were nine more cities with screenings ahead of the documentary's fall release: New York, Chicago, and Los Angeles in the United States; Beijing, Shanghai, and Shenyang in China; and London and Paris in Europe. He also had a showing in his hometown of Akron with a red carpet and the full premiere treatment. At each, there were Q&As with LeBron and accompanying media interviews. It was as extensive of a promotional tour as any summer blockbuster would have gotten. Riding high on the results in Toronto and the demand from distributors and fueled by Nike's support, it was as much publicity as any documentary could have ever dreamed of.

For LeBron and Carter, it was an example of how they could work celebrity, storytelling, demand, and their partners to assemble a major project. In the end, though, it was not a moneymaker. The critics after Toronto weren't as kind, and the audience didn't embrace it much. Despite all the press, they didn't rush to the theaters to try it out. In all, *More than a Game*'s worldwide box office came in at just $950,000. It was nominated for an Independent Spirit Award, which is a significant honor, though it did not win. The accompanying book written in LeBron's voice by Buzz Bissinger, titled *Shooting Stars*, fell flat despite an excerpt in *Vanity Fair*. Bissinger distanced himself from the project, and when it came out in paperback, the title was changed to *LeBron's Dream Team* and Bissinger's name was stripped from the cover.

The struggle to transfer the excitement from Toronto to theaters and make it more of a commercial hit was disappointing. But LeBron and his group walked away with some money from the bidding war for the distribution rights and lots of education about the process.

Going to the Allen & Company conference was another step in that direction. Carter and LeBron had learned that people who were big in media wanted to be in business with them. Businessmen and people in the entertainment industry sometimes lent LeBron their private jets to help further a relationship or to get a meeting.

Brian Grazer, one of the most successful Hollywood producers of the last twenty-five years, was such a fan of LeBron that he reached out to Carter to try to set up a meeting. He brought his young son, who was also a big fan. After a couple of meetings with Carter and LeBron, they hatched an idea for a movie project set around the concept of LeBron running a fantasy basketball camp.

Grazer brought in a few established writers and the project was announced via an article in *Variety* like it was a vehicle for Tom Cruise. Here was one of the most powerful men in show business—Grazer was coming off *Cinderella Man, The Da Vinci Code*, and *Frost/Nixon* at the time—seeking out LeBron and wanting to make him a movie star. This was not a unique concept—athletes had been making movies for decades—but LeBron and Carter were looking at it as a way to be part of the business. It wasn't just about acting; it was about controlling and profiting from the entire process. *More than a Game* was a first step; this would be the next big one. Grazer's *Fantasy Basketball Camp* was put on the books to be shot in the summer of 2010.

Then there was the reception he got in Sun Valley, where LeBron was treated frequently like the biggest star on the premises. He'd just won his first Most Valuable Player Award. The previous season Nike had also launched a new campaign in which LeBron played four different versions of himself and showcased some acting ability, creating some buzz about him expanding into a movie role.

Competing for championships in the NBA was challenging. LeBron hadn't been able to climb that mountain to that point. Recruiting athletes to represent had intense competition, too. Finding successful businesses to invest in could be like finding a needle in a haystack. But when running a production company, often the creators would bring the ideas to them. LeBron and Carter would have to be patient, but they could select from a pile. That had some serious appeal.

LeBron had been adding some quality endorsement partners to his portfolio. A relationship with Steve

Stoute and his New York marketing agency, Translation, had been bearing fruit. Working with Stoute, Carter had closed a major deal with State Farm in 2008. It led to some Super Bowl commercials that featured LeBron, Mims, and Paul. State Farm was looking to connect to a younger audience and picked him to be one of the faces of that effort. The deal Carter closed also had significant charity components: State Farm would donate money to renovate basketball courts in LeBron's name.

By the time LeBron went to Sun Valley, Carter and Stoute had entered serious talks that ended up landing him a multiyear deal with McDonald's. Carter had been talking to McDonald's for nearly four years, and Stoute helped make it happen—LeBron made more than $3 million annually. They kicked off the partnership with another Super Bowl commercial, reprising a classic Michael Jordan–Larry Bird ad where they'd played HORSE against each other for a Big Mac.

Carter had also reopened the door with Microsoft, doing a deal to have a video game on the company's Xbox platform developed around LeBron. They'd gotten larger offers to have him be on the cover of more established games made by EA Sports and 2K Sports. He'd described this choice to students at Harvard Business School as part of a case study to show how he and LeBron wanted to make partnership deals. Carter had multiyear offers that would have paid around $350,000 for using LeBron's likeness on the video game. Instead, Carter took $250,000 per year in a deal from Microsoft that would allow LeBron to participate in the profits, making up to 20 percent, depending on how the brand-new game performed. It was all about equity and control.

All of it had led up to the most important deal Carter would negotiate or, as he explained it to me at the time, "the deal I've been working toward my whole life to make."

That was to make a second deal with Nike. LeBron had signed a seven-year deal in 2003, which would expire in the spring of 2010. Since that time not only had Carter replaced Aaron Goodwin as the lead negotiator for LeBron's marketing deals, but he'd worked inside Nike for several years. He would be going up against some of his old co-workers and sitting opposite the table with one of his mentors, Lynn Merritt.

The first six years of LeBron's shoe sales were good but not great. According to industry analysts, revenues from his signature shoe sales were typically less than $100 million in the United States annually during those years, though he also generated millions in sales internationally that helped him reach some bonus clauses in the deal. Overall, that is a good business, but it was not the second coming of Michael Jordan.

By comparison, the Jordan Brand at Nike was pulling in more than a billion a year in sales during the 2000s and had crossed into more than $2 billion a year by the 2010s, according to industry analysts. Jordan gets a portion of the gross sales, racking up tens of millions each year in royalties.

"The Michael Jordan situation was so unique, it probably couldn't be replicated," said Rick Anguilla, a former vice president at Nike. "It's like the second man on the moon. It's not the same."

Nike was happy with LeBron and was eager to re-sign him. But this time there would be no all-out bidding war and no record contract. Nike wasn't willing to increase his annual guarantee, which was $11 million, dramatically. There was an option to extend the deal, but Carter preferred to negotiate an entirely new contract, in part so LRMR could establish itself as the agent for the deal and be able to collect a commission. Even though LeBron had let former agent Aaron Goodwin go years earlier, Goodwin was still getting a commission on the Nike deal because he'd negotiated it.

It helped the talks that LeBron's shoe was enjoying its best-selling season. In year 6, the design had been a hit with younger consumers. In all, Carter spent eighteen months talking to Nike and assembling the renewal. In early 2010, before LeBron was to hit the free agent market, the sides ended up settling on an eight-year contract that would eventually earn him more than $100 million.

For Nike, a mature multinational corporation that had nearly $20 billion in sales by 2010, there would be no equity grants. What Carter wanted, though, was to negotiate a profit participation package so that the better Nike did selling the shoe, the better LeBron would do.

The contract came at the right time. With the momentum from winning two MVP Awards, LeBron entered a prime period where his popularity and shoe sales would boom. By 2013, the shoes crested the $300 million mark in annual sales. They went even higher the next few years, industry analysts said, returning tens of millions of dollars to LeBron in royalties.

By 2010, between Nike, Coca-Cola, State Farm, McDonald's, Upper Deck, Beats, and Microsoft, LeBron's annual endorsement earnings neared $40 million. *Forbes* labeled him the third-highest-earning active athlete behind Tiger Woods and Kobe Bryant. Carter had led extensions or renegotiations of the existing deals and put together new ones, creating a stable situation for LeBron. But LRMR essentially got out of the marketing business for other athletes, which never took off as they'd hoped. Rich Paul left LRMR and moved to a job at CAA working with agent Leon Rose. Carter and Wachter developed a plan to outsource some of LeBron's marketing.

With long-term deals in place with partners, Carter hunted for new business. The lure of going into media with more gusto was strong, and it led Carter and LeBron down a path to one of the biggest moments on the media landscape anyone had ever seen.

Chapter 9

# TAKING MY TALENTS

On a morning in February 2010, Tiger Woods walked into a ballroom at the clubhouse at TPC Sawgrass in Ponte Vedra Beach, Florida, and apologized for a series of infidelities in his marriage that had become public over a three-month period following a car accident at his home. He read from a script, standing behind a simple lectern and in front of a blue curtain. There were a few dozen people in the room, including family and friends and a couple of hand-picked journalists. After speaking for fifteen minutes, Woods left the podium without taking questions and hugged his mother, who was seated in the front row and in the perfect sight line of a camera that was positioned to capture it. It was carried live on the major networks and all the cable news channels, getting maximum exposure.

LeBron James and those in his circle took notice.

LeBron had a passing relationship with Woods. They'd met at a game when LeBron was in Orlando to play the Magic, where Woods had courtside seats for years before the scandal. They exchanged cell phone numbers, Woods punching in LeBron's number on the old-fashioned flip phone that would end up getting him into so much trouble when his wife got hold of it and found incriminating messages. As two of the highest-profile Nike athletes, LeBron and Woods were connected but not friends. LeBron did have friends across the entertainment and sports landscape but not the golf world. But that wasn't the reason the group was interested in the Woods controversy. It was the way he handled the sensitive announcement.

More than three hundred media members covered Woods's remarks, making it one of the biggest stories in sports at the time. But instead of dealing with that circus, Woods and the PGA Tour sent almost all of them down the road to a Marriott hotel, where they had to watch his speech on a closed-circuit feed. It infuriated some of the media, and the Golf Writers Association of America staged a boycott. But it enabled Woods to control the presentation of the entire event and not be pressed to open up on topics he didn't want to talk about.

By staging it at the PGA Tour's headquarters, he was able to have their staff handle and, in some respects, pay for some of the logistics. This wasn't a proud moment; Woods's reputation was taking a major blow. But despite that, Woods and his management team had found ways to maximize leverage because of the intense demand for capturing his first comments. Some public relations experts stepped forward and slammed the concept, saying among other things that calling a press conference but not allowing the press in alienated those who would be shaping the narrative after it was over. From the perspective of LeBron's camp, it was an eyebrow-raising way of managing a major announcement.

It was around that time that Maverick Carter began to consider how LeBron would make his free agent announcement the following summer. He was in his seventh season with the Cleveland Cavaliers and was coming to the end of his contract. For the previous two years teams had been lining up their pitches and clearing space on their books and rosters to offer him a $100 million deal. Teams in major markets, like the Knicks, Nets, Clippers, and Bulls, were planning to go after him, increasing the stakes even more. When LeBron had extended his contract in 2006 the announcement was handled with a phone call to reporters. The stakes and the interest on this free agency were much higher. Carter and LeBron had spent the last several years looking for ways to capture or even manufacture value that emanated from LeBron's name, likeness, and influence. When he made up his mind in free agency the announcement was going to potentially have huge value. Giving it away in an open press conference or announcement, they thought, could be a missed opportunity.

While he realized there was a symbiotic relationship between media and star players—exposure to his activities and his charity work helped increase valuable awareness and drove sales—sometimes the way the media profited off LeBron irritated him. So why not try to control and profit from something that was so clearly his own? It could be said this was just good business instinct.

Public perception had to be considered, however. If LeBron were to straightforwardly sell off his announcement, there might be a public perception issue. This had always been something they were sensitive about. Back in the early days, when they called themselves the Four Horsemen and were staging relatively low-rent productions like for-profit parties for up to $300 a head, they always made sure to say that a portion of the proceeds went to charity.

They'd gotten a lot more sophisticated in the years since, both with the stakes and with the charities. Nonetheless, donating money to charity was both a good deed and tended to grease some negativity surrounding any off-court cash grabs. And selling the free agent announcement, as Carter was contemplating, fit in this category, even if it represented a strategic power move.

Bottom line, the idea was to use the announcement to raise money for charity, creating a bevy of benefits, both real and perceived.

These discussions and ideas had to remain secret and not interrupt the season LeBron was having. He was entrenched in his prime years, and the Cavs attracted major interest, adding an aging but still eye-ball-drawing Shaquille O'Neal to the roster that season and then making a midseason trade to bring in former All-Star Antawn Jamison. The team won 62 games and got the number one seed in the postseason, and LeBron finished off a breathtaking campaign with his second MVP Award.

When he accepted the honor at the University of Akron's Rhodes Arena, he invited fans in to watch. After a huge ovation when he took to the podium, he said, "I love Akron; it will always be my home and always be my life." That led some to conclude there's no way he'd leave the Cavs, and therefore Akron, in free agency. That, it turned out, was an incorrect assumption.

Nonetheless, some in LeBron's group were quietly considering concepts. Initially, some of the discussions about how to approach the free agency centered around LeBron taking a tour of the cities he was considering, which opened the door for some marketing opportunities. Nike stepped forward and made a public statement denying they were planning to create a different colorway of LeBron's shoe for each team he was considering after reports surfaced to the contrary.

Ultimately, all that was penny ante. One thing that could be said for LeBron and his closest friends was they always thought big. In some ways, it had gotten them to where they were. Breaking out on their own back in 2005 was absolutely thinking big. When it came to that first free agency, as the hype built, they just went bigger.

What we're talking about here is *The Decision*, which aired on ESPN on July 8, 2010. It was the biggest business play LeBron and Carter had ever made. And it resulted in perhaps the lowest moment in their career.

If you've read to this point, it's fair to say LeBron's business operations had stops and starts in the five years since he and Carter had created their own business. There were some incredible highs. Money was rolling in. There were offers everywhere. And they were learning ways to find deals that both enriched them and excited them. They had gone from having their toe in the media world to wading in to their waist. Pulling off a primetime special would put them in another echelon not to mention increase their visibility. If nothing else, it would be historic for sports. No one had ever seen anything like it.

It accomplished none of that. Instead it set them back years.

What is unfortunate is that the concept was, from a certain perspective, ahead of its time. When looked at through that lens, one of athlete empowerment and controlling the message, it's actually aged quite well. Whether it's high school stars announcing their college decisions or other NBA stars making their free agency choices, *The Decision* changed the way business was done. It is now commonplace for an athlete to handle a transactional announcement through a controlled media experience, which is the technical term for what *The Decision* was. Some are handled better than others, but without question the show changed the environment and what's accepted. That's the rough legacy of *The Decision*, though it is mostly unsaid and uncredited because no one wants to attach themselves to it.

Had the show been executed differently, it might've turned into a proud moment in Carter and LeBron's career, one in the game-changer column. Instead, it was a ball and chain around the group's ankle for years. And even coming up on a decade later, it remains like a pebble in their shoe.

The concept truly got going during the 2010 Finals. LeBron and the top-seeded Cavs had been ousted in the second round by the fourth-seeded Boston Celtics. LeBron had played poorly in several of the games, notably a game 5 loss at home that essentially cost his team the season. Afterward, he went underground, cutting most of his communication with the team and anyone else.

He reappeared, oddly, just at the start of the Finals to do an hourlong interview with Larry King on CNN that revealed next to nothing other than a complete lack of chemistry between the young basketball star and the veteran talk show host.

A few days later, on a Sunday night, Carter was at game 2 of the Finals in Los Angeles. The Lakers were playing the Celtics, who had used their victory over the Cavs to springboard them into the championship round. At halftime of the game, Carter was approached by Jim Gray, the well-known broadcaster who had become famous over the years for scoring major newsmaking interviews with the likes of Muhammad Ali, Pete Rose, and Kobe Bryant, among many others. Gray had done a few interviews with LeBron. He interviewed him the night he was drafted. He was on the sidelines for LeBron's first NBA game. He had a relationship, but it wasn't that close. Still, Gray always had been aggressive as a reporter. At halftime, Gray marched down from his seats to the floor, going straight to talk to Carter. He hadn't come to the game that night with this as a priority, but when he saw a chance, he went for it. What he wanted was to press Carter to try to lock down the first interview when the free agent choice was made. Carter was interested but noncommittal.

Gray didn't land major interviews over the years by not closing. He didn't let Carter off the hook with a maybe. He put forth an idea. Gray suggested LeBron and LRMR buy time on a network and announce it that way. Sell the ads themselves. Control the broadcast themselves. And, of course, let Gray be the host. That, it must be said, was thinking big.

"I have to say it wasn't like this was incubating in my head," Gray said. "I just said it in the moment. It was an idea."

Because it was a Lakers game and there were some giants in the media industry right there, it went from concept to reality very quickly. Carter and Gray happened to be with Ari Emanuel, the Hollywood agent and co-head of major Hollywood agency William Morris Endeavor, in some courtside seats. When Emanuel heard the idea, he got excited and told Carter he should do something like it.

Carter had been in L.A. talking with David Geffen, the billionaire media mogul, who also attended the game. When he heard about it, he endorsed the idea as well. Carter had a true affinity for Geffen, fostered when he read a book about him called *The Operator*, which had been published in 2000 (ironically, Geffen hated the book and disavowed it after originally cooperating). Carter kept a copy on his office bookshelf. He'd been introduced to Geffen previously by Jimmy Iovine, Geffen's longtime collaborator at Interscope Records. The chain of relationships just kept on going.

Carter had met with Geffen about a crazy longshot plan. The L.A. Clippers were one of the teams that had cleared salary-cap space to try to sign LeBron that coming July. LeBron had some interest in playing in Los Angeles and was intrigued by their young star Blake Griffin. But he was never going to sign with the team while it was owned by Donald Sterling, a notorious NBA figure who was loathed by many of his players, coaches, and employees over the years. Geffen was interested in buying the Clippers—many L.A. businessmen had been over the years—and a plan was hatched such that they might be able to leverage LeBron's free agency into getting Sterling to sell a controlling interest.

The concept, generally, was that Sterling would sell at a likely record price and then LeBron would commit to signing with the club, instantly raising the team's profile and value. There have been worse ideas, and it would have been the ultimate power play move, a free agent forcing an ownership change. The NBA probably would have backed it; then commissioner David Stern was no fan of Sterling and had hoped for years he would sell the team. But Sterling declined, as he always did, and the idea died. (The NBA eventually forced Stern to sell in 2014 after racist comments became public.)

Even having the conversation was a heck of an affirming moment, one of the biggest names in Hollywood trying to move hundreds of millions just to get into business with you. With these sorts of stakes, it wasn't surprising that Carter and LeBron's egos about their deal-making power in the media world had been swelling. LeBron had been invited to attend the game that night but passed because he knew it would have become a sideshow with his free agency pending. So instead Carter sat with Emanuel and just down from Jeffrey Katzenberg, Geffen's partner along with Steven Spielberg in DreamWorks. Oh, and Tom Cruise was there too. It was L.A., after all.

Carter asked Emanuel if he could pull the deal together to put a special on TV. Already the parties knew they might not even have to buy time. Tiger Woods didn't need to buy time to control his message. If LeBron was willing to give the announcement exclusively to one network, they probably wouldn't have to buy anything at all. While LeBron's basketball business was handled by Emanuel's archrival, CAA, his group had used Emanuel's company to make the distribution deal on *More than a Game*. The conversation continued over dinner after the game. By the next day, it was a legitimate project being pursued by Emanuel and WME. With the intense interest in LeBron's free agency and the considerable weight that Emanuel could throw around, it was going to happen.

"I got a phone call from Maverick and Jim Gray, and I'm pretty sure I was the first person they contacted. Then I talked to Ari," said John Skipper, who was ESPN's vice president in charge of content in 2010 before becoming the company's president. "They told me the idea and the charity element. They weren't being cynical about the charity; they were serious about it. But I think everybody understood that provided some cover. I was in charge of all the content on ESPN, and I had the ability to give them an hour. And that's what we did."

ESPN wasn't crazy about Gray hosting it. Internally, there was pushback when the idea made its way around the corporate offices. He'd previously worked at ESPN but left the network. Emanuel, though, insisted Gray do the interview, and that's the way it went. Emanuel and Skipper went over details at length, and an agreement was reached. ESPN wasn't slowing down, eager to have the exclusive on one of the biggest news stories in recent memory.

Emanuel enlisted one of his executives, Mark Dowley, to help put the special together. Dowley lived in Greenwich, Connecticut, one of the most affluent communities on the East Coast. He also had access to a private jet and felt the proximity to the airport in White Plains would allow LeBron and his party to slip in and out of the area easily. He suggested they hold it at a Boys and Girls Club in the community. LeBron had benefited from Boys and Girls Clubs when he was young, which made him interested in helping the charity. Also, it was a national operation, and money could be split among several cities to widen the reach.

As was standard business for LeBron, he went to

his partners. Nike was willing to make a donation but didn't want to take a visible position on the show, which ended up looking like a shrewd decision. Coca-Cola and Microsoft did get involved, buying ad time. VitaminWater and Bing, Microsoft's search engine, became cornerstone advertisers. The only advertiser who was outside the LeBron universe was the University of Phoenix, which bought the most ad time but donated some of it to the Boys and Girls Club. These sales were very good; in all, around $4 million was generated, which is tremendous for any hour, much less one that didn't have a live sporting event.

The entire thing was put together in about a month, which is unusual for any project of this magnitude but especially for a one-of-a-kind show like this. There was no precedent. There was no producer who had experience pulling it off. Unlike Woods, who had gone to the PGA Tour to help him with his announcement, LeBron didn't go to the NBA to ask for support. When Stern found out, he thought it was a terrible idea. He tried to stop it. He called Skipper—ESPN was one of the league's television partners—to try to talk him out of it. Then he called back again.

But there was no stopping *The Decision*. It seems that Carter and LeBron might have made a classic mistake those on the rise have made for generations: They were so focused on what they *could* do that they didn't fully consider whether they *should* do it.

That probably went for Emanuel and WME at the time, too. Even for an established agency that had packaged plenty of television shows and movies over the years, this was new territory, and getting to new territory first was a win in this business. It was grabbing control of the biggest sports network at 9 p.m. on the East Coast, and then selling the sponsorships themselves and embedding them into the program. It was a supreme flexing of might and, in theory, a possible new way of doing business.

When it came to the actual show, it turned out there were many flaws. After meeting with six teams—the Heat, Clippers, Knicks, Nets, Bulls, and Cavs—the previous week, LeBron spent the afternoon of the show at Dowley's house in Greenwich after flying in from Cleveland. Instead of only focusing on the performance, he needed to film an ad for the University of Phoenix as part of the deal. Then he got a surprise visit from Kanye West, who was in New York and found out where LeBron was and came up to hang out with him before the show. Dowley had hoped to keep the location quiet, but there was no chance of that happening, especially with the logistics of producing a live television show at the local Boys and Girls Club.

The news was out quickly, and by the afternoon of the show there were reports that LeBron had chosen Miami. But social media was in its infancy in 2010—in fact, LeBron didn't join Twitter until that very week—

and news moved slower. Though several outlets had reported where LeBron was headed, the news didn't seem
to be as ubiquitous as it would have been had it been
two or three years later, when news spread instantly
through social media channels. That explains why the
announcement may have landed hard on many who
hadn't prepared themselves. Or even if they'd heard,
they didn't believe it.

The setting was a somewhat antiseptic and darkened
gym with some kids silently in chairs in the background
next to VitaminWater machines, which was odd. There
was no energy in the room whatsoever, just tension,
and it spread to the viewers. There was some curiosity
about the location, so close to New York City and two
of the teams that were bidding on him.

"It was a million small decisions put together that
looked bad. But there was a reasoning and a logic
behind every small decision," said Ellen Lucey, an executive at Coca-Cola who worked with LeBron. "I think
we needed more time. But there are some things you
only see in hindsight."

Gray had a list of questions he'd gone over with Le-
Bron, Carter, and Leon Rose, LeBron's basketball agent
who would put together the deal the next day. He didn't
know for sure what LeBron's decision would be. But he
knew it wasn't going to be re-signing in Cleveland, that
much was clear.

Gray ended up asking questions—eighteen of them,

if you want to be exact—to build to the moment and to draw the audience. This was one of the most irritating aspects for the viewers, that the suspense seemed to be artificially extended. More than ten minutes passed between when ESPN tossed from its studio to Greenwich. This delay was later criticized as being interminable, but it actually was a compromise. Initially the idea was to wait even longer and to go to commercial before coming out with it. Gray asked some scripted questions and some off the cuff, including if LeBron still bit his nails when he was nervous. Meanwhile, LeBron was practically shaking in his seat, he was so nervous.

Gray asked LeBron how many people knew what his choice was, and LeBron said you could count them on one or two hands. That wasn't completely true. For example, the pilots and crew of the two private jets waiting for LeBron and his entourage had been briefed; they had to file a flight plan and needed to know whether to get fuel to fly to L.A. or Chicago or Miami. And there were plenty of others by that point, too.

Just as Gray asked him if the teams had been informed of his decision, I got a text message from Cavs owner Dan Gilbert. He was telling me that the Cavs had been told LeBron was signing in Miami, and he encouraged me to publicize it to undercut the show. It was far too late for that. There were more than 10 million people watching at that point. I had only about 30,000 Twitter followers in those days, and none of them were looking at the app in that moment. I'd known for hours LeBron was likely headed to Miami and posted a story to that effect on the *Cleveland Plain Dealer*'s website. Gilbert had just confirmed that LeBron hadn't had a change of heart, which I thought was possible considering the stakes and what he was about to do, so I was not surprised when LeBron uttered the words: "This fall, I'm taking my talents to South Beach."

Two things crossed my mind at this moment. One was how LeBron always referred to Miami as "South Beach." If the Cavs had a game coming up against the Heat he'd say, "We have to play them in South Beach this week" or "The Heat are tough to beat in South Beach." The Heat didn't play in South Beach. It's close, yes, but they're different areas. It'd be like saying you had dinner in Manhattan when you were actually in Queens. The second was that "taking my talents to" was how Kobe Bryant announced he was going to the NBA in a press conference back in 1996 when he stood indoors on a podium with sunglasses perched above his eyes on his forehead.

But much of the huge TV audience was aghast. So was the audience in the room, for that matter. There was no clapping, only murmurs of surprise and collective gasps. It was as if a standup comic had just told an offensive joke. The children, apparently doing what they were told, didn't make a sound. He was going to Miami to create a super team, and in a coarse way he'd just let the world know. "Taking my talents to" wasn't even an original line, but it was instantly branded as folly.

"I was just shocked he didn't have a better prepared remark," Skipper said. "He put himself in a difficult spot saying that."

"The advice that he received on this was poor," Stern said a few days after it aired. "This decision [show] was ill-conceived, badly produced, and poorly executed. Those who were interested were given our opinion prior to its airing."

Fans in Cleveland were hurt, naturally, that their hometown hero had decided to play elsewhere. There probably wasn't a way LeBron could have delivered a message to Cleveland and Akron that would have been well received, though he didn't do a good job of trying to make it understood. The television show just seemed to make it worse.

Ten months later, after LeBron beat the Celtics in the playoffs in his first year with the Heat, he emotionally spoke about his feelings for the first time. He said, "I knew deep down in my heart, as much as I loved my teammates back in Cleveland and as much as I loved home, I knew I couldn't do it by myself against [the Celtics]. The way it panned out with all the friends and family and the fans back home, I apologize for the way it happened. I knew this opportunity was once in a lifetime. To be able to come down here and pair with two guys and this organization."

Had LeBron said something like that immediately before or immediately after he announced his plans, there's a chance some of the strong backlash might have been muted. But he wasn't in the frame of mind that night. For as good as his instincts had been about basketball and business during his career, *The Decision* was tone deaf. The concept might have been next level, but the anticipation of the reaction was as big of a misread as LeBron has made in his life. He knew he'd be upsetting some fans that he didn't pick their team. He had no feel for the sort of anger it would incite or how the way the broadcast was presented would only make him and his group an easier target.

No one seemed to be more angry than Gilbert. Within two hours, Gilbert released a letter to Cavs fans that became nearly as infamous as *The Decision* show itself. Among other things, it called LeBron "our former hero," "narcissistic," and "former king" and the show itself a "cowardly betrayal," a "shameful display of selfishness," a "shocking act of disloyalty," and a "heartless and callous action."

When the letter arrived in my inbox from the Cavs it was stunning. Each line seemed to be more vicious than the previous. I couldn't believe it was an actual official statement. Part of the reason is that it wasn't formatted like most team statements were; instead it was in enlarged Comic Sans font. Anyone who had ever received a private email from Gilbert would know that this was his preferred method.

Much more could be said about Gilbert's choice to publish these thoughts and has been. What is relevant to note before moving on is that Stern rebuked LeBron for the show but left it at that while he fined Gilbert $100,000 for the letter.

As for the show, much of the audience turned away after the Miami announcement. There had been discussion of a plan to present a $1 million check to a representative of the Boys and Girls Club so that the audience would be reminded of the purpose of this endeavor. That never happened for reasons that to this day not everyone seems sure about. As a result, many don't remember that *The Decision* ended up being a massive fund-raising operation.

In all, more than $2.5 million was given to more than fifty-nine Boys and Girls Clubs across the country. A partnership with HP helped get a thousand new computers into clubs. A larger portion of the funds were sent to the clubs in the cities involved: Miami, Cleveland, greater New York, Chicago, Los Angeles, and Greenwich. New roofs were installed, courts were refurbished, and the like. Had these endeavors been highlighted in the first ten minutes of the show, the impact could have been different. The reaction to the choice may have been the same, but it would have imprinted differently.

Instead, much of the intention of the thing wasn't just lost to history; it was lost in the moment. When stories came out months later about what the money was doing for the local clubs, it was buried in the fray or dismissed as trying to put lipstick on a pig.

The rest of the program contained some pre-filmed segments with LeBron in Akron at his high school and an interview between LeBron and ESPN analyst Michael Wilbon. But in general, it was a blur. The blur continued the following night when he joined new teammates Dwyane Wade and Chris Bosh in an extravaganza announcement at AmericanAirlines Arena in Miami when he infamously predicted that the Heat would win as many as seven championships. In fairness, he was playing to the crowd inside the arena, which was eating it up. These were very different TV shows; the Heat produced the second, but James was blamed for the poor taste in both for years.

A week later, ESPN itself lampooned LeBron at its annual sports award show, the ESPYs, the same show LeBron had hosted a few years earlier. A skit with actors Steve Carell and Paul Rudd aired during the show with Carell, playing the LeBron role, announcing: "I'm taking my appetite to Outback Steakhouse." It was one of many instances of past allies turning on LeBron.

As the fallout was spreading, LeBron and the rest of the group became furious with ESPN. They felt the network hadn't supported them in the immediate and distant wake of the show after they'd been partners. During the Wilbon interview, viewers were shown images of fans burning LeBron jerseys in Cleveland. LeBron gave a reasoned response, which was that he wasn't making an emotional decision but was making a business decision, and that if the shoe was on the other foot no one would have felt for him if the Cavs had decided to cut him. This comment came off as cold as Cleveland's raw emotions were pouring out. For most of the next season, LeBron declined to do one-on-one interviews with ESPN before and after nationally televised games in what amounted to a silent protest.

The damage, though, was done. Two months later, the Q Scores Company, a firm that measures how the general population views public figures, announced that LeBron's so-called Q rating had taken a massive hit. Compared to eight months earlier, when the previous polling on him had been done, people who viewed him in a positive light decreased by 42 percent while those who viewed him in a negative light increased by 77 percent. The results could be spun in various directions, but without question, it was a huge hit.

It was hard to quantify exactly why this happened other than that people just simply hated the way the show came off. There may have been a fragment of the audience who resented him going to Miami, which was a flashy choice but not a serendipitous one. But largely it seemed that the way LeBron handled his announcement was viewed as egomaniacal and insensitive. There may have been a racial element at play, too. The Q Scores report showed that while his positive rating among African Americans dropped from 52 percent to 39 percent, LeBron's negative Q rating only went from 14 percent to 15 percent. The takeaway was that within the black community, more people were neutral to LeBron than negative.

The media, which had largely been shut out of the process, amplified the fallout through round after round of vicious criticism. LeBron was routinely booed in road arenas, even in places that didn't have any perceived skin in the game, like Memphis, Atlanta, and Portland. The following season his two-year run of MVPs was broken when Derrick Rose took home the honor. LeBron's stats took a bit of a dip as he merged with new teammates, but he saw losing to Rose as a penalty for *The Decision* because media members vote on the award. He came back and won it again the following two seasons and owned Rose and his Bulls in the playoffs during that span.

LeBron and his group still have mixed feelings about it all. Going to play basketball for the Miami Heat was a great choice—there was never a regret there. The team made the Finals four consecutive seasons, and LeBron won his first two titles. Despite what the Q rating said, 2010–11 proved to be the best year to that point for his signature shoe sales. His jersey shot to number one in sales in the league. And ratings for Heat games were regularly the best among all teams. Not to mention all the money they sent to charity, which made real and immediate impacts on children.

How were they supposed to take that data? These were all things they'd been trying to accomplish all along. They were achieving goals and creating new horizons. Even with all the backlash, Carter's visibility in the media business and with power brokers had increased. As they huddled into their proverbial bunker to assess the damage, they found it hard to truly admit they were sorry. The program didn't look good, and the way it was presented was bad—they accepted that— but the foundational concept had matched exactly what they'd hoped. It was the best of times; it was the worst of times.

One significant casualty of *The Decision* was the movie project LeBron was working on with Brian Grazer. The film, which had switched from being called *Fantasy Basketball Camp* to *Ballers*, had been announced by Universal and Grazer's production company. A director had been hired, and it was given a 2011 release date with filming scheduled to begin in the summer of 2010. In the wake of *The Decision*, however, the movie was delayed and ultimately shelved.

Dealing with it all in a higher-profile situation than even he was used to, LeBron took it badly. He was used to being well liked. He'd had failures on the court, and he'd been roundly jabbed for his poor play in the play-offs the previous year. But he'd never been treated this way. Worse, he allowed himself to take it in. He was an avid reader and television watcher, and he saw what was being said.

Even as the Heat rattled off wins in his first season, LeBron was so stung by the criticism that it changed his personality. At one point, using his new Twitter account, he wrote: "Don't think for one min [sic] that I haven't been taking mental notes of everyone taking shots at me this summer. And I mean everyone!" Other times he'd post hateful and even racist messages people were sending him via social media. This may have been some attempt to create a measure of sympathy, but he was on a backfiring streak, and it only seemed to make people realize that messages they thought were getting sent into the void were actually getting through. The volume increased.

LeBron found it hard to let his guard down, refusing even to accept lighthearted ribbing by peers. When Anthony Tolliver, a role player, signed a two-year contract with the Minnesota Timberwolves for a relatively pedestrian $4.5 million that summer, he put out a video mocking *The Decision* and saying "I'm taking my services to the north." LeBron bristled, saying, "I heard about it. I know we play Minnesota twice." For a joke, that was out of character, too.

However, this angry version of LeBron wasn't his

true self. He tried at times to embrace it. Once, during his first year in Miami, LeBron played a brilliant game in Portland. He scored 44 points and was a wizard defensively, leading a comeback win. The crowd that night had been vicious in their booing—Portland was another place where he didn't expect to feel hate, but it rained down anyway—and after the game he threw up his hands.

"I've kind of accepted this villain role everyone has placed on me," he said that night. "I'm OK with it. I accept it."

But he wasn't. The next day, after I'd written a story to this effect, Carter called me. He wanted to know why I'd written it. I told him it was because LeBron had said it himself. Carter said that he disagreed and that wasn't what LeBron needed to be saying or feeling. He and Rich Paul approached LeBron and talked him down, and a few days later in L.A., LeBron took back his words. The root of all that was *The Decision*; he bore it every day for more than a year. It wasn't until late 2011 that he came out of his fog, promising to get back to himself.

But he's always carried the scar.

"You know, I thought we were doing something cool, something interesting. I still feel that way to this day," Skipper said. "At ESPN we have games, we have news shows, and we have entertainment shows. This was an entertainment show. I personally made the decision to put it on. And in retrospect, I just think it was ahead of its time."

Skipper and LeBron share that viewpoint. On this one, the regret is complicated. But it was impossible to sell that in 2010, and it remains challenging now.

"There had never been anything like it," Gray said. "And there will never be anything like it ever again."

At the time, LeBron and his group didn't have the benefit of waiting to see how history judged *The Decision*. It left them reeling, and it ended up forcing them to reevaluate things. It ended up as a turning point for his business career.

# Chapter 10

# MOGUL

When executives from Fenway Sports Group sat down at a meeting with Maverick Carter in Paul Wachter's office in Santa Monica in the fall of 2010, they didn't totally know what they were doing there.

FSG was a power player in both sports and marketing, and Carter was taking meetings with companies that may want to represent LeBron James for marketing deals. LRMR, the company that had been formed to do just that, was diversifying. Rich Paul had decided he wanted to become an agent, and he left LRMR to work under LeBron's agent, Leon Rose, at CAA. Paul planned to focus on recruiting players to the agency as LRMR had abandoned that pursuit for the most part.

Away from the floor, LeBron had started to devote more attention to media and entertainment. Even with the movie project falling through, he went ahead in

developing a cartoon series where he played four different characters called *The LeBrons*, based on a series
of Nike commercials that had been popular. Some of
the marketing deals that LRMR had done for LeBron,
namely State Farm and McDonald's, had been aided
by outsiders, notably Steve Stoute. Now, LRMR was
looking for more assistance.

That framework all made sense, but the issue was
FSG didn't represent individual athletes; they represented or flat-out owned major brands and sports teams.
The primary owner of FSG is John Henry, a hugely
successful former commodities trader, but he has more
than a dozen partners. One of his most important is
Tom Werner, a successful Hollywood producer who
happened to be very close friends with Wachter. As is
his custom, Wachter had already connected Carter with
both Henry and Werner when they met at a Berkshire
Hathaway conference, Warren Buffett's annual gathering of shareholders. But for Wachter to make a deal
happen here was going to take some creativity.

FSG bought the Boston Red Sox in 2001 in a complex
deal that Wachter had assisted on. Werner had been a
longtime part-owner of the San Diego Padres. Henry
was the controlling owner of the Florida Marlins and
also had a small piece of the New York Yankees. There
were a lot of moving parts to sort through, which, just
to make it more convoluted, also included ownership
involving the Montreal Expos. When it was over, Henry

had the Red Sox, and Werner was in the ownership group with him, acting as the chairman running the team's TV business.

In subsequent years, FSG had taken part-ownership in Roush Fenway Racing, a NASCAR team, and in 2010 had just executed a $480 million purchase of Liverpool Football Club. That was a challenging deal, too; Liverpool's previous owners had gone bankrupt, and Henry had bought the team from a bank in a bidding war. Wachter helped with that deal, too. Add in their ownership of NESN, the regional network that broadcast Red Sox games across New England, and it was an impressive portfolio. What business, however, could they do with LeBron, a star athlete who was a big brand but not a team?

"Paul has a pretty incredible gut when it comes to putting together partnerships," said Sam Kennedy, FSG's president and CEO. "He made it clear to us that LeBron wasn't just a player, he was a franchise himself. And he and Maverick had an unusual and frankly brilliant plan. They were thinking about the long haul and about the value of sports clubs. They said they'd forgo a traditional arrangement and make a smart bet on John and Tom's ability to run Liverpool with the same success they'd run the Red Sox."

That was, essentially, Wachter's pitch. Still licking their wounds from *The Decision*, Wachter and Carter assembled a deal that merged the major priorities they'd developed over the previous five years: to take something intrinsic, the ability to monetize the simple desire people had to be in business with LeBron, and cross it with value, to squeeze as much possible cash out of each deal by capturing something that is worth more than just a defined paycheck.

Fenway would get the rights to go out and pitch LeBron to make marketing deals and would be able to pocket a percentage. Plus, the company would be able to add LeBron's name to their portfolio of assets—though, in their home base of Boston, where LeBron had been a major rival with the Celtics, the public reaction would be a little interesting. In return, LeBron and Carter would receive a small percentage of the just-acquired Liverpool FC. It would end up being about 2 percent of the franchise.

To be frank, without Wachter and Werner's friend-ship, there's no way it would have happened. It was a pretty generous deal, though it isn't normal for an athlete in their twenties to be satisfied to be let into the purchase of an English soccer club. This is where Carter and LeBron being mature for their age in comprehending value showed itself. Of course, with-out LeBron's immense popularity, there's no way FSG would have been willing to allow LeBron to have equity, which is as valuable as beachfront property. It still took negotiation throughout the winter and into the spring of 2011. But it remains one of the more unique deals an

American athlete has ever made, trading ownership in a sports team for marketing rights.

Shortly after the deal closed, LeBron made a trip to Liverpool to watch a match at Anfield, the club's legendary stadium. A meeting was arranged with the team's players. LeBron brought gifts for all of them. If you've gotten this far in this book you know what it was: special edition Beats headphones for all of them to wear and be seen wearing.

Shortly after the LeBron-FSG partnership came together, they had their first marketing deal with Swiss luxury watchmaker Audemars Piguet. It was a small deal, worth less than $1 million annually, but it was just the type of international marketing pact that the partnership was designed to find.

Naturally, Wachter was involved in this one as well. Arnold Schwarzenegger, Wachter's original client, had been marketing the high-end Audemars Piguet watches since 1998, and he and Wachter had a long history with the family-owned company. In 2013, the watchmaker released a special edition with LeBron's name on it that retailed for $51,500. Only six hundred were made.

In 2012, FSG made a deal with LeBron and Dunkin' Donuts. This was also a bit of an in-house collaboration as FSG handled Dunkin's international marketing. The deal lined up LeBron to pitch Dunkin' Donuts and Baskin-Robbins ice cream in China, Taiwan, South Korea, and India. It was the type of connection both parties liked: Dunkin' leveraged LeBron's popularity in Asia, and LeBron found a seven-figure international deal. Fenway later helped put together deals with Samsung and Progressive insurance (after LeBron's deal with State Farm ended).

LeBron's end has worked out beautifully. By late 2018, *Forbes* had valued Liverpool FC at $1.9 billion, four times what Henry and his partners had paid just eight years earlier. That meant the stake LeBron and Carter received had soared along with it, making it worth more than $30 million at those prices. This came in addition to the money LeBron made on the endorsement deals FSG found for him. It was indeed a brilliant deal for LeBron, yet another reason Wachter has been valuable to his business development over the years.

While FSG executives maintain that the deal has worked out well for both sides, it's unlikely the firm earned as much on commissions as LeBron's growing equity in Liverpool became worth. Part of the issue was that LeBron became less interested in the type of endorsement deals the company was set up to land for him. The high-end watches and Chinese deals were beneficial, but LeBron and Carter frequently passed on similar offers to seek out more ways they could land ownership.

One of the great benefits of being involved with FSG was it put LeBron and Carter into business with Werner and allowed for a deepening of the relationship over time. They ended up getting into another venture together in 2012, when LeBron and Carter had joined Werner in an investment into a startup chain restaurant franchise called Blaze Pizza, along with Maria Shriver and her son, Patrick Schwarzenegger. When deciding whether or not to join the group, at least as LeBron tells the story, he visited the original location in Irvine, California, and sampled the pizza at the Subway-style design-your-own-pie outlet. When he approved of the process and the product, he decided to buy in.

Yes, Wachter helped put that deal together, too. In addition to the investment, LeBron got franchise rights in Miami and Chicago and opened more than twenty locations within five years. This was a more traditional investment than the deals LeBron had done in the past. Though the company benefited from his association, it wasn't as formalized as the marketing arrangements he'd had with Beats.

That changed in 2017. Blaze was growing quickly: *Forbes* said it was the fastest-growing restaurant chain of all time when it expanded from two locations to two hundred within four years. Wachter and Carter saw a window and made their kind of deal.

LeBron's endorsement contract with McDonald's was at an end that year. This was a lucrative arrangement with a legacy brand, the sort of thing LeBron and Carter sought out the previous decade. McDonald's offered an extension for $15 million over the next four years, which was very good money and required only a few days a year of LeBron's time. But Blaze was willing to boost LeBron's stake in the company to add "brand ambassador" to his list of duties. That sounds cooler than "spokesman." And Blaze had plans to go international, which would open more markets where LeBron could invest. Plus, naturally, the deal came with more equity than he'd originally bought in for. Jordan had been with McDonald's for years and collected millions. LeBron, Carter, and Wachter were thinking about tens of millions.

"I think for me, it was like, 'Oh wow, we get to actually build this.' Forget the money, we could actually build something. And if it doesn't become successful, then I can only blame myself," LeBron said on a podcast, on his Uninterrupted platform, of course, in announcing the deal. "I was like, 'Who doesn't like pizza?' I don't know a person in the world who doesn't like pizza."

Within the group, there's a belief that the Blaze investment could surpass the Beats windfall in the coming years. And LeBron's promotion in his expanded role has mostly been using social media and the media platforms he owns. He didn't even have to spend days approving and then making commercials. As for the $15 million they left on the table with McDonald's, they don't even remember it anymore.

With the FSG and Blaze deals locked in, the relationship with Werner continued to be both important and valuable, especially as the group looked to get more into the type of business that Werner made his name in, which was producing content. Werner is one of the most successful television producers in history. He often is attached to his two biggest hits: *The Cosby Show* and *Roseanne*. But he has a litany of success including *A Different World, Grace under Fire, Third Rock from the Sun, That '70s Show,* and others. Baseball was always his side business. When he was an owner of the Padres, he helped get Roseanne Barr to come sing the national anthem before a game, and her infamous rendition is remembered to this day.

In 2013, Werner called Carter with an idea for a television show based on an NBA player. Again, let's pause here for a moment. Here we have a hugely successful producer wanting to include Carter and LeBron in a project despite their very limited experience working in entertainment. They'd produced *More than a Game*, which was emotional and enjoyable but not particularly successful. They'd also produced *The LeBrons*, which had a dozen five-minute episodes that aired on YouTube. Their big studio movie project was on ice.

In the meantime, Carter had been heavily involved in the promotion for a new company called Sheets Energy Strips, which was a caffeine-infused strip that dissolved on the tongue meant to get in on the market owned by energy drinks like Red Bull and 5-Hour Energy. The company, which Carter and LeBron of course had equity in, had assembled a $10 million marketing budget and built it around the catchphrase "take a sheet." Before the big game, LeBron would "take a sheet." Music artist Pitbull, who was part of the company as well, said he'd "take a sheet on stage." *Adweek* called it the worst campaign of the year. The company ended up failing. OK, no one bats 1.000; there are winners and losers. But Carter and LeBron were still learning.

But because of their business ties and because Carter had impressed Werner with his ideas and his way of doing things, Werner was reaching out. They worked on the idea, Carter added to the concept, as did LeBron, and Werner went out to pitch studios and networks. Here was Werner, who had been a producer for more than fifty shows dating to before Carter was born, taking the idea through Hollywood.

This was how *Survivor's Remorse* was born. That was the name of the TV show the collaboration of Werner, Carter, and LeBron created. It ended up being the project that changed LeBron's business focus for good and fast-tracked the growth of SpringHill to be the driver of his off-court focus. It goes without saying at this point in the story that Wachter played a major role, too. Carter told Wachter about the idea while they were on a snowboarding trip.

The plot resembled the backgrounds of LeBron and Carter: a star from an impoverished neighborhood makes it in the NBA and brings his childhood friend with him to manage his affairs. They face challenges dealing with family members and friends from their hometown whom they've left behind. Wachter was intrigued by the idea, so he did his thing: He put them together with Chris Albrecht, a television executive at Starz that he'd known for years. After some pitch meetings, Starz bought the series. Wachter ended up joining LeBron, Carter, and Werner as an executive producer on the show.

The key to the idea was that LeBron wasn't in the show; he would just influence it and market it. That brought things to a new level. If that process could work, then it would open up a world of opportunities. Ultimately, LeBron was a basketball player first, and the majority of the time he was focused on it. He couldn't be a full-time producer or even a part-time actor. He did make a guest appearance on *Survivor's Remorse*, but that was it.

The idea was to use LeBron's popularity, which was rebounding from *The Decision* after he started winning MVPs and titles, while he was still in his prime to set up long-term options after his career. They'd also made strides on the media front, having hired a new media strategist named Adam Mendelsohn, who had crafted a plan to rehabilitate LeBron's image. He quickly became a valued member of the inner circle. The connection was made by—wait for it—Wachter. Mendelsohn had been Governor Arnold Schwarzenegger's deputy chief of staff and communications director before going into the private sector.

Getting *Survivor's Remorse* on TV helped make LeBron and Carter's hopes of creating a media empire seem like it could be a reality. So did the quality of the show, which ended up running for four seasons, successful by any measure in Hollywood. It had a small but devoted viewership and critics loved it, especially the way it took complex issues and made them feel authentic and funny. It was Carter and LeBron's first true victory in this area, not unlike when they partnered with Cannondale years earlier. That fueled their interest in leveraging LeBron's name to get into investment deals. Nurturing this show had given wings to their new interest.

It also led to a significant change in the way they could make things. With SpringHill now a functioning production house, they were able to receive pitches to make shows and not just try to create them. These pitches involved projects that would specifically tie to LeBron and those that would not.

In quick succession, SpringHill started getting an array of shows into production with a growing list of partners. Carter no longer referred to himself as the CEO of LRMR but forefronted his role as CEO of SpringHill as LRMR faded into a back-of-house administrative role in the now churning media operation.

They created a show with the Disney XD network and some ESPN executives called *Becoming*, which detailed the backgrounds of top athletes. LeBron's story was on the premiere episode. They did a reality show for CNBC called *Cleveland Hustles*, which funded and tracked startups in lower-income areas of Cleveland. Then a game show with NBC called *The Wall*, which was a new take on a trivia-for-cash show. They were getting things done, building brands, and making money in the process.

SpringHill's growth was a part of a three-pronged plan leading LeBron's pivot to the media business. These three branches developed independently but grew together.

In 2014, LeBron decided to leave Miami and return to Cleveland and the Cavs. This was obviously a massive moment both in LeBron's career and NBA history. A lot went into it and a lot came out of it, so much so that I wrote a different book on the topic called *Return of the King*, available at fine retailers, should you want to know more about it.

When he made the announcement, the differences from what happened in 2010 were both stark and sublime. Instead of a live TV show, LeBron let the world know his choice via letter on *Sports Illustrated*'s website that was co-written by LeBron and gifted feature writer Lee Jenkins. This was the brainchild of Mendelsohn, who believed it was a better way to control the message and prevent it from being reduced to sound bites like "I'm taking my talents to South Beach."

In all honesty, the basic idea wasn't that different from *The Decision*. Instead of getting a TV network to hand over the reins, a major magazine and website allowed LeBron to take control. ESPN had been vilified for its role in allowing LeBron to do so in 2010; in 2014 *Sports Illustrated* was lauded. The difference was in the delivery.

First off, the news came right out front, not ten minutes in. The headline read I'M COMING HOME. What followed was a flowing, personal, and nuanced explanation of LeBron's choice to go back to Cleveland, buffeted with promises to take it slow and steady. There was no promise of seven championships, as LeBron had done in a flippant but later painful moment in the televised rally when he signed with Miami. With the help of a strong writer and the polish that rounds of editing allow, the end result was more pleasing in every way. It didn't hurt that the story—prodigal son goes home to try to make good—was simply more attractive to the average fan than the last one: mercenary goes to form unbeatable team. It also must be said that LeBron's résumé was quite different; he'd won two championships, and it provided him a certain amount of capital that his 2010 move just didn't have.

In 2010, the group said it hit them how badly *The Decision* had gone when they made the flight down to Miami from Connecticut late that night. The videos of the burning jerseys were out there, and the backlash on social media had started. By the time Heat president Pat Riley and coach Erik Spoelstra met them at the private jet terminal in Miami, LeBron and his associates were a little melancholy. Spoelstra had brought cookies to celebrate; they were looking for hard liquor.

In 2014, they realized just how well it was going over on the flight after the letter came out. LeBron had made the announcement from Miami and signed the contract with the Cavs that evening before he took an overnight flight to Rio de Janeiro, where he was doing some Nike business around the World Cup Final. As the Nike Gulfstream jet headed south over the Caribbean and the high-end red wine was cracked open, the group started talking about the reaction and what it could teach them. Like with *The Decision*, it was really about athlete empowerment. LeBron had something he wanted to say, and by going directly to the fans he was able to create a connection that, this time at least, had paid off. Was this something that could be replicated?

Lynn Merritt was on the flight. So was Mendelsohn. With Mendelsohn's background in politics, creating a message and getting it out was a daily part of his job. LeBron's letter in some way was like a political speech, an announcement followed by a platform. Mendelsohn, who was a partner in a public relations firm, was also keenly aware of the trends in media and the direction things were going. The use of digital media was growing rapidly, moving away from traditional outlets, especially for younger consumers. It was one of the reasons Mendelsohn wanted to use a digital outlet, *Sports Illustrated*'s website, instead of a traditional outlet, like ESPN TV, to make the announcement.

One of the lines in the essay read: "I'm doing this essay because I want an opportunity to explain myself uninterrupted." That was the basis for the concept, to present something without it having to be filtered or chopped up by media or reduced to a character limit by social media. To be uninterrupted. On the flight, the group came up with a plan to create a digital media platform that would allow athletes to do what LeBron had just done: deliver a message uninterrupted that would be easily shared via social media. If they could profit off these stories by selling them to brands or getting them sponsored, all the better. They decided to name it exactly that: Uninterrupted.

They weren't alone in having the idea. As Uninterrupted was developed over the coming moments, a similar concept was being assembled by Derek Jeter and his representation agency, Excel Sports Management. Less than a week after Jeter retired from the Yankees in the fall of 2014 after a brilliant career, he announced the formation of a website called the Players' Tribune, which would be a place for athletes to publish personal essays just as LeBron had done with *Sports Illustrated*.

Excel had a number of the world's best athletes under its umbrella, a ready-made list of contributors. Within eighteen months the idea was backed by some athletes and investors as it raised $18 million in funding, including an investment from Kobe Bryant.

Uninterrupted had a huge name in his prime, LeBron, and they had the vision of Carter and Mendelsohn to help foster ideas. But they also had a very valuable connector: yet again, Wachter.

In addition to all his other connections and roles, Wachter had been on the Time Warner board of directors since 2010. One of the largest media companies in the world, it controlled a number of influential media brands including Warner Bros., Turner Sports, HBO, and Bleacher Report. As LeBron's SpringHill and Uninterrupted ventures grew, it would largely be through strong connections and investments from these Time Warner entities stemming from relationships that were developed with guidance from Wachter.

Carter recruited and signed a number of high-profile athletes and gave them ownership shares in the new platform, and they contributed video testimonials. Some of the initial partners were Rob Gronkowski of the New England Patriots, Draymond Green of the Golden State Warriors, and UFC fighter Ronda Rousey. The videos showed up on Bleacher Report through a deal negotiated with Turner Sports. The first ambitious project was a documentary series with LeBron and

Green as they led up to playing against each other in the 2015 Finals.

As all of this was unfolding, there was the third pole in this operation, which was LeBron's acting work. He'd done some commercials and small work where he'd been the voice of characters. Plus there was that *Saturday Night Live* gig, but that was years in the past.

The first major, legitimate role came in the comedy *Trainwreck*, which filmed in the summer of 2014. Comedian Amy Schumer wrote LeBron into the script mostly because he was the most famous basketball player she knew, not because she thought he'd actually take the role. But when actor Bill Hader was cast as the lead, the possibilities opened up because Hader had worked with LeBron at *SNL*. Hader and Judd Apatow, the director, showed LeBron the script and took him to lunch.

LeBron and Carter didn't love it at first. The script called for LeBron to have a relationship with Hader's character, a doctor, because of a knee surgery. Carter didn't want LeBron to be portrayed as an injured athlete in the movie; he'd never had knee surgery. Apatow and Schumer changed the script and made LeBron a best friend character to Hader. Amar'e Stoudemire, who did have a history of knee injuries, had no issues playing the injured athlete.

LeBron had no history as a bankable movie star. Having him in a supporting role in the movie wasn't a guarantee of selling tickets. Apatow could have just moved on to another basketball player willing to have scenes in a hospital gown. Carter and LeBron knew there was a power in saying no at first. Apatow, Schumer, and Hader were so motivated to work with LeBron, though, that they were willing to change numerous scenes to make it work. And Schumer and Hader set him up with some winning lines in the script.

With that, LeBron was sold on the project, and he came to New York for a week of filming in the summer of 2014, shortly after he signed with the Cavs. They set up the shooting schedule so LeBron could film his scenes last. Again, it helps to be a very famous basketball player. And, apparently, to be selective and demanding in projects can pay off. Somewhere along the line, LeBron and Carter had learned these lessons. It didn't always work, but it often did.

When the movie came out in 2015, LeBron won critical and audience acclaim for the role. Apatow and Schumer had given him just the right amount of exposure in the film. There were some layup jokes without sounding corny or going overboard. In short, it was pitch perfect and the exact way to be introduced into movie acting, not too big or too small. It opened up a world of opportunities down the line.

He was hardly the first major athlete to get into acting. From Jim Brown to Wilt Chamberlain to Shaquille O'Neal, many had come before him. But none of them had visions of doing it as part of the studio. Thanks to Wachter and Carter, that's where LeBron was going to try to be different.

Putting Uninterrupted's first videos on Bleacher Report was just the appetizer of the deals with Time Warner. In the summer of 2015, just as *Trainwreck* was about to hit theaters, Carter finalized yet another important deal. The Nike deal had been revolutionary. The FSG deal had been creative. This one was wide-ranging. It was a multiplatform agreement with Warner Bros. that would put LeBron and Carter in a position to create content for every screen.

As part of the pact, Warner Bros. would fund some of SpringHill's development costs and enable Carter to add staff to help ramp up production. They gave LeBron and Carter a cottage on the Warner Bros. lot in Burbank, the so-called Warner Village that had once been the setting for the *Gilmore Girls* TV show. More important, Warner Bros. got the rights to any films and TV shows that SpringHill would produce plus any digital media shows. These were the types of all-encompassing deals Hollywood moguls like Clint Eastwood, J.J. Abrams, and Ben Affleck had with the movie studio. And they didn't make TV and digital shows like SpringHill had on the assembly line.

Within a few months another layer was added: Turner Sports and Warner Bros. combined to invest $15.8 million into Uninterrupted to fund the expansion of staffing and projects. Time Warner had invested deeply in what had now become a full-fledged content operation that Carter had built with LeBron as the vehicle, Mendelsohn as a contributing voice, and Wachter as the dealmaker. It was quite the acceleration. This was the kind of thing Carter and LeBron could only have dreamed about ten years earlier when they contemplated taking control of the off-court business interests. This was the kind of machine that could turn LeBron's worth from nine figures into ten.

Time Warner executives seemed to like Carter, who had taken the time to build relationships with David Levy, who ran Turner Sports; Jay Levine, who ran the Warner Bros. TV operation; and Richard Plepler, who ran HBO. They clearly wanted to be in business with him and LeBron. But they also may have wanted to try to get LeBron into their family to help make *Space Jam 2*, which had been a desire of movie executives for more than a decade. And it was a property owned by Warner Bros.

As far back as 2012 people were trying to get LeBron to reprise the role Michael Jordan had played in the first *Space Jam* movie, which was released in 1996. In 2014, a movie executive reached out to me looking for advice on how to approach LeBron with a version of the project that he'd be willing to make. That producer was hoping to get it made by 2016, the thirty-year anniversary of the original. That didn't happen. After LeBron's successful turn in *Trainwreck*, it didn't happen. Carter and LeBron heard pitches, read scripts, and workshopped the idea of *Space Jam 2* for years. If such a project ended up as a hit, it could make the studio hundreds of millions and be worth every investment in a LeBron side project.

Just like when they sat down to consider the Reebok deal back in 2003 all the way to their meeting with Apatow in 2014, it took more than just money to get LeBron and Carter to sign on to something. "Always think big" had been one of their mantras, and with Wachter as a valued ally, it made lots of things possible.

Sure, LeBron could have signed on to do *Space Jam 2* right after *Trainwreck*. It would have been well received and he would have gotten a lot of money for it. But why do that when there was a wide-ranging deal from Warner Bros. that could help set up several of their media businesses for years of success? Finally, in 2018, when the deal with Warner Bros. had been reupped, LeBron and Carter agreed to a script, a producer, and a director to make *Space Jam 2* with initial filming planned for 2019. Carter and LeBron will be executive producers.

In the meantime, Warner Bros. and HBO had green-lit more than a dozen television and digital projects for SpringHill to develop as they looked to find a hit or two. Liverpool FC reached the Champions League final as new rights deals helped its annual revenue increase to more than $460 million and its profit to more than $50 million. Blaze Pizza set a target to have five hundred stores open by the end of 2019.

It had been a long, long journey from selling $50 admissions to nightclub parties.

"For me, I try to never make any of my decisions about what is the most money," LeBron said. "I think about building things. That's what we've been doing, building."

# Chapter 11

# I PROMISE

It was a brilliantly sunny late June day in 2006. LeBron James towered over flocks of children as he pedaled through the streets of his hometown alongside several of his Cleveland Cavs teammates who came to ride in support. The kids all wore T-shirts proclaiming their participation in the King for Kids Bikeathon, all of them having raised at least $100 to be donated to charity as part of the day.

Parents stood behind rope lines and barricades taking photos. Police closed off streets to traffic across the city so riders could breeze toward the finish line in downtown Akron. It was all about raising money while promoting physical fitness and also donating some bicycles to children who didn't have them. Microsoft streamed it online. What a terrific event.

Only LeBron's foundation, the primary benefactor

of the day, lost money on it. It lost money the year before, too. The bikeathon also was a drain on the city's coffers, because the city has to pay for overtime for police and other workers to provide support. It was great for families and was inspiring for kids, which in the end is maybe all that mattered. But from a business perspective, it was a write-off.

In his early years in the NBA, LeBron had to learn how to play with the rigors of his schedule. He had to learn how to recover, finding routines for treatment and rest. In his business, he had to learn who he wanted to work with and how to set up his support system. And he also had to learn how to be a philanthropist.

Right from the start, LeBron knew he wanted to have his charity work based in his hometown of Akron, and he wanted it focused on children. He often found himself relating more to children than adults. Many adults wanted things from him and looked to exploit or profit from him. In kids he found a peace and a purity. In his first years in the NBA, he was closer in age to some of the children his foundation was working with than he was to some of his own teammates. He remembered his struggles as a child, fighting through poverty and periods of being transient.

In 2004, he launched the LeBron James Family Foundation to do exactly that. But athlete foundations routinely struggle, especially in the early going. According to a report in the *Boston Globe*, baseball star

Alex Rodriguez's foundation, for example, gave only 1 percent of the foundation's proceeds in its first year to charity and later was stripped of its tax-exempt status. Athletes from across sports often mean well but are too busy to follow through, leaving their foundations understaffed, or they are victims of fraud.

For the first three years LeBron had a foundation, it operated in the red. The bikeathon, which was a tremendously positive annual event, was a culprit. Doing such a big event without enough sponsorship cost more money than it raised. After two years, the event was suspended (it did come back in a different form later) and LeBron replaced the staff he had running the foundation. Then one of the volunteers who worked with the foundation ran a scheme using the foundation's name and letterhead to create an event at a waterpark that ended up costing $13,000. The goal was for LeBron to not just write checks but to multiply giving by involving partners and the community. But this is a complicated mission and, in the early years, it didn't work. After replacing all of the foundation's staff in 2007, he laid them all off in 2009 and outsourced the operation of the fund.

Some of LeBron's endorsement contracts had a charity element and allowed him to steer funds toward causes. Both Sprite and State Farm would rehabilitate community centers in LeBron's name, and he guided some of that money toward charities at home. He also typically would help renovate a community basketball court or children's learning center as a part of the All-Star Weekend. He also put money into his own charity, covering the operating costs. His foundation still made significant donations even if it didn't operate efficiently. But it was unfocused and not reaching its potential.

According to federal tax documents filed in 2011, the LeBron James Family Foundation gave away just $89,000 to various programs that year. That's not an insignificant sum, nor is it an indication of LeBron's overall charity work. The year before, thanks to *The Decision*, he gave away more than $3 million to charity, mostly the Boys and Girls Clubs. There were also the funds from his endorsement deals that he guided. Yet eight years into his career and then with deep pockets and huge influence across both the sports and business worlds, LeBron had allowed his foundation to largely just go through the motions.

But in 2011, something changed for LeBron in a very profound way. State Farm, one of his partners, launched a nationwide program aimed at keeping children from dropping out of school, a growing issue in underprivileged and economically challenged areas. It was called 26 Seconds, named because studies showed that every 26 seconds a child dropped out. When he heard about it, LeBron was stunned.

"It's a staggering statistic," he said. "You would

never think in your wildest dreams something like that happens. It was a no-brainer for me to be part of it. I could've been a statistic."

This number hit him where he lived. In fourth grade he'd missed more than eighty days of school because of instability at home. His mother had trouble keeping the family in one place and was dealing with some of her own problems. He'd been taken in by a family in fifth grade, the Walker family, and they changed his life. With a stable support system, routines, and accountability as a part of his daily life, he had perfect attendance in fifth grade. He became a good student who cared about school. LeBron suddenly saw what he needed to do with his resources and connections: directly reach into the lives of at-risk children, children who were like he was.

This lightning bolt hit him at an interesting time, a moment when he was reevaluating his life to a degree. He was in his second year in Miami, hardened emotionally by intense backlash to his free agency decision. He was so beaten down by the scrutiny that surrounded him that it broke him in a way. He spent days in isolation after losing in the NBA Finals. As he pondered why he was so hurt and why he hadn't been able to perform well—his play in that Finals was substandard, and he was a reason why the Heat lost, and it was not something he was used to—he realized he was too worried about outside opinions. He was too worried about what people thought and what they tweeted and what they said on television.

When he came back for the 2011–12 season he had a new outlook on life. In that first season in Miami, his girlfriend and two sons didn't join him, instead staying back in Akron. He saw them but not as often as he'd been used to. When it came time to start the new season, he asked her to move to Miami so he could reunite the family. She agreed but under two conditions: that he make a commitment to her and that her parents come with her, because she wanted her boys to be near their grandparents. On New Year's Eve 2011, LeBron got down on one knee and proposed to Savannah Brinson. Her parents moved into his house with her.

The following March, LeBron made another major decision. Along with his teammates, he posed for a photo wearing hoodies to protest the death of a Florida teenager named Trayvon Martin, who had been shot wearing one. LeBron and teammate Dwyane Wade helped convince the team they could make a strong statement, since they were the most famous team in American sports at the time. It was a hot-button political issue. The man who had killed Martin, George Zimmerman, had claimed self-defense. It involved race, class, and the Second Amendment. LeBron shared the photo on his social media, creating awareness. Martin had died nearly a month earlier, and the story was gaining traction but hadn't fully hit the mainstream. LeBron and the Heat helped it become a national story.

In the past, some athletes had shied away from making major political statements because it naturally offended some of their fans. LeBron had campaigned for Barack Obama in 2008, but a majority of NBA players tended to be Democrats, so supporting the Democratic nominee wasn't taking as much of a risk. In fact, in the NBA, supporting a Republican can often create more tension, at least within the locker room.

But LeBron had a sensitive political moment in 2007 and elected to stay on the sidelines. One of his then Cavs teammates, Ira Newble, led an effort to draft a letter to the Chinese government condemning its support of the Sudanese government despite the genocide that was taking place in Darfur. The team was about to play in the NBA Finals, and Newble wanted to take advantage of the platform.

Newble felt it was an important time and place for this particular humanitarian fight. The coming Olympics in Beijing were applying some pressure to the Chinese on the world stage. LeBron, however, did major business in China with Nike, and that complicated the situation. Criticizing the government in China in any way had the potential to compromise that business.

In the end, LeBron didn't sign the letter, the only Cav not to. He said he needed to gather additional information and research the topic before making a commitment. That may have been a responsible answer. But it was seen as a cop-out, and LeBron took some criticism for it, some of it reaching the political media, which he wasn't used to being targeted by.

The choice called to mind Michael Jordan, who famously stayed away from political issues during his career. In 1988, he declined to back a Democratic candidate in a statewide race in his home state of North Carolina. He was routinely credited with saying the line "Republicans buy sneakers too" as his reasoning for not making the endorsement. It's unclear if Jordan ever actually said these words. But his neutral stance said enough: He wasn't interested in taking a stand that had the potential to turn off a large part of the consumer base. Jordan is a billionaire today because of his mass marketability and because his shoes continue to sell decades after his retirement. If he stayed out of politics for business reasons, it seems to have worked.

In 2012, with Trayvon Martin on his mind, LeBron left the sidelines for good on political matters.

"For me I think it's just a sign of growth," he said about the decision in an interview several years later. "I don't know if this was the moment that sparked something for me to speak up on social issues. What I like to talk about, I have to be educated about issues. I think it all starts from an individual being comfortable in their own skin and knowing who they are."

LeBron had reached that point. With a massive voice

and huge social media following that he could speak to without the filter of media, LeBron began weighing in on political issues. On police-related deaths, like Eric Garner, Alton Sterling, Philando Castile, and Tamir Rice. Against Los Angeles Clippers owner Donald Sterling for being racist. Eventually against President Donald Trump. And many others in between. His shoe sales have never matched Jordan's and likely never will. But his political impact has far outpaced Jordan's.

This awakening spurred a new way he was going to work with his foundation. He put a trusted employee, Michele Campbell, who had been one of the original LRMR employees back in 2006, in charge of the foundation. With a new guiding principle to attack dropout rates, Campbell worked with educators to try to identify some root causes in Akron. Campbell was an excellent choice to work on it. She had a doctorate in education and knew the field. She was also one of the very few that LeBron trusted, meaning she had the power to get him to believe in ideas.

LeBron moved his offices from Cleveland, where LRMR famously held LeBron's free agent pitch meetings with six teams the week of The Decision, to Akron so his staff could be more connected to the city. They also deepened a partnership with the Akron Public Schools, a relationship that would start to grow in important ways in the following years. LeBron had

202 • LEBRON, INC.

provided support to children in the system for years, but it was often at surface level, handing out supplies and backpacks and sponsoring occasional events. This was something totally different.

In Akron the dropout rate among high school students was 26 percent, one of the highest in the state of Ohio. The foundation learned that the issues start long before high school, that third grade was the time when if a child was behind in reading or math that their chances to graduate high school plummeted. That's where the foundation, Campbell believed, should start its intense work.

With Campbell as the leader and the schools as the guide, the foundation created a program. It started with two hundred third graders, two hundred of the kids whom the district believed were most in need. Then, the plan went, each year a new class of third graders would be added as the older students were tracked.

The foundation would provide funding to give the students special attention. They would get extra instruction and be tracked and supported. In short, it was an effort to plug the cracks these children were starting to slip through. At first, the program was called Wheels for Education, an evolution from the bike rides to working on programs within the schools.

Later, the program was renamed I Promise. One of the important roles LeBron would play would be to attempt to motivate the children. He couldn't be there every day, so a system was devised to make his presence felt. One of the core parts of the plan was a pledge that the kids in the program would be encouraged to recite. A promise. This is what it was:

> *I promise to go to school, to do all my home-work, to listen to my teachers, because they will help me learn.*
> *To ask questions, and to find answers. To never give up, no matter what.*
> *To always try my best, to be helpful and respect-ful to others, to live a healthy life by eating right and being active.*
> *To make good choices for myself. To have fun.*
> *And above all else, to finish school!*

In turn, LeBron made his own promise back to them. LeBron's promise was:

> *I promise to never forget where I came from.*

To reinforce the message, LeBron started wearing a rubber bracelet every game that had the phrase "I Promise" on it. Children were provided with matching ones so they could feel connected to him when they saw him play on TV. The foundation put life-size cutouts of him in some schools with his promise on them to help create the connection. For encouragement, some children would get a call with a recorded message from LeBron.

After sending out $89,000 in grants in 2011, LeBron flooded money into his foundation. In 2012, it gave out more than $750,000. In 2013, he doubled it again and made it $1.5 million as he was able to draw more sponsorships. He also announced he was donating $1 million over three years to his high school so it could renovate its gymnasium. By 2016, the foundation was giving out more than $3.5 million per year in grants.

Campbell taking over the foundation was a significant factor in it becoming more aggressive and involved. But it was LeBron's passion being ignited that fueled the growth. It also didn't hurt that he'd signed some major deals: a $100 million deal with the Miami Heat in 2010; the second Nike deal, which was paying off with the increase in sales of his signature shoe and sending him more than $20 million annually; and, of course, the Beats windfall. He was wealthier than he'd ever been, and he was sharing this wealth by increasing his giving in his community.

But what sent the foundation to the next level was LeBron applying what he learned by working business deals. It's one thing to make a straight transaction; it's another to leverage name and fame. If LeBron could use businesses' desire to be attached to him to drive a favorable equity deal or make a movie, was there a way he could use this from a charity perspective? It wasn't just in the private sector that companies wanted to be attached to LeBron's name.

This led to two projects that would vastly change the scope of the foundation and alter how LeBron was viewed across the country. In 2015, the foundation made a historic deal with the University of Akron, a large state institution located in the city's center. It helped that Campbell worked at the university for thirteen years and had deep connections there. It may have helped that at the time the university's president was embattled and facing public relations problems (he resigned after just two years on the job). But really it was about a concept that was so remarkable that the parties had to find a way to make it happen.

By this point there were more than 1,100 children in the I Promise program, and the initial class of third graders would soon start high school. More third graders would be coming every year. LeBron thought about what happened after he helped get them through high school. The mission had been conceived to prevent dropouts. But there were bigger goals to be achieved.

Here was the deal that was put together: If members of the program were able to get good enough grades and test scores, the University of Akron would agree to provide them with a full four-year scholarship. That was potentially up to two hundred free rides the university was willing to fund every year, starting when the initial class of third graders that had pioneered the program reached college in 2021.

For his part, LeBron agreed to help the university with fund-raising and some other promotional projects. The school would rename its School of Education after the foundation, hoping that some students would choose to become teachers and go back and educate at-risk kids in their hometown. Having LeBron's name on a building at the university certainly had value, and the other end of the deal was very attractive to the foundation.

At the start, the idea was to try to get more students to have a chance at a productive life by getting them through high school. It became a moonshot idea, a huge swing in an attempt at generational change. It was ambitious and creative and something LeBron could have never dreamed of doing just a few years before. They got a new big-name partner, JPMorgan Chase, to offer some corporate support of the program. So did LeBron's legacy partners Nike and Coca-Cola.

He announced it at a big event for his I Promise kids at an amusement park in the summer of 2015. The children, then all in elementary school, didn't seem to comprehend what had just happened. They also couldn't really understand the value of what he was doing for them. But the adults, mostly parents, in the crowd certainly did.

There was a bit of a misconception after the announcement became public that LeBron was funding these scholarships directly. Some media outlets did the math and made the assumption he was going to spend $40 million of his own money to send the 1,100 children to the school himself. He got good press for that, to be sure.

That wasn't the case. LeBron certainly could afford to give out many scholarships by just writing checks. Doing it this way, with a partnership, enabled a lot more children to be involved. He was using his influence to multiply the deal. Indeed, he got huge credit for it, probably more than the university, on a national level, though there was some irony in it. His efforts to send millions to charity with *The Decision* had largely been overlooked. This grand deal he brokered with the college ended up getting him credit for donating fewer actual dollars. Perhaps it was all some public relations karma. All that, however, was less relevant than the work being done.

Later the foundation added several other programs, including one to help the parents of children in the program to get their GEDs so they could extend the reach to entire families. Then, with a gift from Sprite, it launched an institute to help prepare high school students in the program for college so they had a better chance of success when they eventually arrived on campus.

Over the following three years, the foundation kept growing and kept pushing. It would be years before the success of the program could be quantified. It was the type of investment school systems dream of, and there was a real effort made to try to make it a model for other cities and perhaps other philanthropists.

After extending their partnership with the Akron Public Schools, another major step was taken in 2018 when LeBron opened the I Promise school. This was a brick-and-mortar elementary school that would implement the program every day, giving children full-scale attention. It started with 240 children in third and fourth grade. The demand to get in was so intense that a lottery system was used.

A major investment from the foundation was required. It spent $2 million to get it started, including renovating an existing school building, and then pledged up to $2 million per year to help with operating costs. This money went to supplement staffing, food, and programs at the school, which would have a longer school day and longer school year than other schools in the district. The students were given breakfast, lunch, and a daily snack. There was a food bank at the school for families in need. There were free bikes and helmets for students who needed them. The school is slated to eventually grow to 1,000 students and have grades 1–8.

"This is a huge moment not only in my life, in my family's life and the foundation's life, but in these kids' lives as well," James said as he opened the school in

July 2018. "As a kid from Akron, I remember walking these same streets. When people ask me why a school, that's the reason why. I know what these kids are going through. I know their dreams. I know their night-mares. I know what they're going through. That's why this school is here."

The 2016 championship he won in Cleveland, break-ing a fifty-two-year championship drought for the city, is his basketball legacy. The school, LeBron hopes, will be his personal legacy in his hometown.

His charitable work extended beyond the schools. In 2016, he donated $2.5 million through the foundation to the National Museum of African American History and Culture in Washington, DC, for an exhibit on the life and work of Muhammad Ali.

As he got older, LeBron started to feel a kinship to Ali, who made a mark not only for his athletic career but also for being a political activist. The donation helped create a relationship with Ali's family. That same year his SpringHill production company made a deal to create a documentary on Ali with HBO.

His affinity for the boxing great was stoked by Lynn Merritt, the Nike executive who remained in his inner circle throughout his career. Merritt later became a board member on the LeBron James Family Founda-tion's board. He is from Louisville, near where Ali grew up. Merritt appreciated Ali from a young age and helped pass that admiration on to LeBron, sometimes bringing recordings of Ali's fights with him on the road to watch in LeBron's hotel rooms during the playoffs.

The hope is that this will only be the beginning. The foundation will look for more ways to invest in children. The scholarships and the school are big projects that will require real support, maintenance, and money to keep growing. His commitment to it seems to be as strong as anything he's ever done.

There are a lot of things LeBron wants to accomplish off the basketball floor over the coming decades. But as he looks to add zeros and influence, one of the biggest lessons he's learned in business over the last decade is a different way to define prosperity.

"There was a time when I was a kid when it was just like, there's no way I'm going to be able to get out of this situation. I just thought about that every day," LeBron said. "I had dreams and I had mentors and they allowed my dreams to become who I am today. People can talk about everything else besides that, but they can never take away what I'm able to do for my hometown and people all around the world. That's what means more to me than anything. The basketball thing, I love it and I enjoy it, but to give back and be able to open up a school, that's something that will last way beyond my years."

# Chapter 12

# L.A.

Anyone who was surprised when LeBron signed with the Lakers in the summer of 2018 on a four-year, $154 million contract probably wasn't paying attention.

After signing the deal with Warner Bros. in 2015 to make SpringHill Entertainment—formerly Spring-Hill Productions—a legitimate Hollywood operation, Maverick Carter moved to Los Angeles. This wasn't a temporary or second home situation; he was going there to stay. He bought a gated $3.5 million house just off Mulholland Drive in Hollywood Hills, complete with a saltwater pool, guest house, wine cellar, and movie theater.

It was part of a developing migration for the Le-Bron operation. Earlier that year, LeBron bought a $21 million, nearly 10,000-square-foot home in Brentwood not far from where Paul Wachter lived, in an $8 million gated estate. In 2016, Rich Paul spent $3 million on a five-bedroom home with a glass-wrapped balcony that overlooked its pool in Beverly Hills. After studying for a few years at CAA, Paul's decision to leave and start his own agency was paying off. He took some clients with him and landed a handful of high-profile players on his own. LRMR didn't get John Wall out of college, but Paul got him as a client and negotiated a $207 million contract. Later, Paul landed two other number one overall picks, Ben Simmons and Anthony Davis. L.A. is the hub of the sports agency business, a natural place to establish a base, and Paul had done just that.

In 2017, while still playing in Cleveland, LeBron upgraded to a 16,000-square-foot home a few blocks away in Brentwood with eight bedrooms, eleven bathrooms, an elevator, a steam room, a pool, and an indoor-outdoor gym. He spent $23 million on that one.

Also in 2017, the Los Angeles Lakers signed one of Paul's clients, Kentavious Caldwell-Pope, to a one-year, $18 million contract. It was more money in a single-season deal than most assumed Caldwell-Pope would receive. It was also a bit surprising, because he had to deal with a twenty-five-day jail sentence for a DUI arrest during the upcoming season, though he was able to miss only a few games because a judge allowed him to be part of a work-release program where he could play games and then return to jail.

But as a result, Paul would end up becoming a regular at games at Staples Center during the 2017–18 season to keep an eye on Caldwell-Pope and make sure everything was in order during the awkward month when he was sleeping in jail while playing for the Lakers. During an early-season game, Lakers owner Jeanie Buss invited Paul to sit with her in courtside seats during the game as they chatted and got to know each other better. Caldwell-Pope is a good wing player who had a reputation for being a scorer and a good defender, a mix that made him somewhat in demand. But it didn't seem like a reach to assume the Lakers had at least a few ulterior motives when doing the deal.

When the move, the third of LeBron's career, became official, there weren't any grand announcements via television show or essay this time; it was simply announced in a press release on Klutch Sports letterhead, Klutch Sports being the agency Paul started in 2013. Within hours of LeBron's announcement, the Lakers agreed to re-sign Caldwell-Pope for $12 million, again higher than some league analysts believed he'd get in the open market.

The migration to Los Angeles was complete. After winning the championship in 2016, LeBron knew he had the capital to leave the Cavs again if he wanted to. When LeBron returned to Cleveland in 2014, he pondered whether he could put himself in a position to perhaps become an owner of the franchise after his retirement. LeBron made inquiries into what owner Dan Gilbert's long-term plans were with the franchise. It is against league rules for a current player to be an owner—Michael Jordan was a part-owner of the Washington Wizards during his second retirement and had to sell his stake in the team before he returned for the final act in his career—so buying into the team or, as LeBron would have preferred, being gifted shares was out of the question. But down the line it wasn't out of the question.

The year before LeBron returned to the Cavs, *Forbes* valued the team as being worth $515 million. The following season they were valued at $915 million, though it must be noted that all teams increased in perceived value at that time in the wake of the L.A. Clippers selling for $2 billion. Looking back, had David Geffen been able to get control of the Clippers with LeBron as leverage in 2010, it would have been one hell of a business move.

*Forbes* estimated that the Cavs' revenue grew more than $40 million per season with James in the fold. That sort of increase in wealth indeed might have been worth a partnership down the line. Those in LeBron's inner circle also believed a referendum that passed in Ohio in 2009 and cleared the way for Gilbert to build casinos in Cleveland and Cincinnati was only possible because of LeBron and how he'd helped vault Gilbert's popularity in the state. That's a matter of debate; Gilbert is a cunning businessman who made smart investments and ran a strong campaign to get the casino issue passed. Nonetheless, the casinos had extended his net worth and could have further incentivized him to become a business partner with LeBron after his playing career.

Gilbert and LeBron's re-pairing had always been tenuous. The letter in 2010 had done irreparable harm, and despite the championship, their connection remained rigid. It took a turn for the worse in 2017 when Gilbert didn't retain popular general manager David Griffin over a contract dispute. Two of Gilbert's primary business partners who were co-owners of the Cavs, Jeff Cohen and Nate Forbes, also had a breakup with Gilbert around the same time.

Then Kyrie Irving, the brightest star Cleveland had ever seen other than LeBron, demanded a trade. LeBron preferred that Irving not be traded, but when Gilbert asked LeBron to extend his contract beyond 2018 so he could operate with the knowledge he wouldn't leave again, LeBron declined. Determined not to be left without a backup plan, Gilbert traded Irving to Boston for a package built around a future first-round pick.

That series of developments greased the skids. LeBron was already eyeing L.A. and saw no way forward with Gilbert. Any long-range ideas of owning the Cavs were pushed off for the time being. The Cavs got back to the Finals for a fourth straight season but were soundly defeated in a four-game sweep by the Golden State Warriors. LeBron had one of the greatest playoff runs in his career even though he was thirty-three years old. For the first time in his career, he played all 82 games. In the playoffs he twice hit game-winning shots at the buzzer and delivered masterpiece performances to help the team win two game 7s, including in the Eastern Conference Finals against the Celtics.

But in the Finals, he got so frustrated during game 1 at a couple of suspect calls by officials and at teammate J.R. Smith losing track of the score at the end of the game that he lost his cool. He burst into the locker room and punched a whiteboard, cracking a bone in his hand. He was able to play the next three games, but he wasn't himself and his tenure in Cleveland ended in an inappropriate whimper.

When LeBron's free agency came a few weeks later, he actually didn't have many great options. In 2010, when he made his first free agent jump, he had the option of staying home in Cleveland, joining the Miami Heat with Dwyane Wade and Chris Bosh, or going to the Chicago Bulls to play with young stars Derrick Rose and Joakim Noah. In 2014, he could have stayed with the Heat but instead joined the Cavs, who had Irving and were soon to trade for All-Star Kevin Love.

This time, things were more complicated. His current team had exhausted its assets and was showing signs it wanted to start a rebuild. The Lakers had cleared their roster to chase free agents and had a handful of mostly unproven young players. Both the Houston Rockets and Philadelphia 76ers badly wanted LeBron, but his family wasn't really interested in living somewhere other than Cleveland or L.A.

By the fall of 2018, SpringHill Entertainment had more than a dozen documentaries, scripted shows, competition series, and game shows either on the air, in development, or in production. They had shows on Showtime, HBO, Starz, the CW, CBS, NBC, and Facebook. LeBron wasn't actively acting or involved in any of them; he was listed as executive producer. It was a functioning production house that didn't need to have him on the screen to get a project made. He also didn't need to have an association with just one network or production house. It was true that his association with Time Warner, perhaps helped by Wachter's role on its board of directors, had been a launching pad. But through Warner Bros., LeBron and especially Carter, who was involved in the day-to-day meetings with talent to find and identify projects, had won the respect of the industry. They had firmed up a reputation; it was much more than just getting a foot in the door because of LeBron's name.

The athlete-generated media platform Uninterrupted, which moved into gleaming new offices in the Viacom building near the historic Hollywood and Gower intersection, had its own slate of more than fifteen projects. They ranged from a documentary on a former NBA player who started his own marijuana business to a film on NBA star Vince Carter that was shown at the Toronto International Film Festival.

Nothing had gotten the critical acclaim of *More than a Game*, which was the brainchild of a first-time director, or their first scripted series, *Survivor's Remorse*, which had been put together by Hollywood legend Tom Werner. None had the commercial success of *Trainwreck*, which ended up making $140 million worldwide, in which LeBron had been a supporting player. Otherwise, the biggest success had been *The Wall*, a game show on NBC that had been extended for several seasons, even though that production was endangered when the host, Chris Hardwick, was put on leave when an ex-girlfriend accused him of abuse. But the bottom line was that LeBron and Carter seemed to have created a small empire that looked to be viable into the future. If they kept getting things to air, they kept up their chances of finding the kind of hit that could vault them into the Hollywood elite. Still relatively early in their entertainment careers, they were performing well and making money. And Warner Bros. was still itching to make *Space Jam 2*, the project that promised to be the big payoff of the entire relationship.

At home, LeBron's two growing sons had enjoyed

their summers in L.A. Both were burgeoning basketball stars. LeBron began to believe his oldest, Bronny,
had a chance to be an NBA player someday. Having
them play in highly competitive high school programs
in Southern California was attractive.

This was the backdrop as LeBron had to consider
leaving Cleveland and skipping a chance to play for
another team, like perhaps the Houston Rockets or
Philadelphia 76ers, that would be an instant contender.
He believed the Lakers might have a chance at drawing
another star in the future, though that would be more
of a risk. It would be a bet on the most glamorous
franchise in the league drawing another great player—
not the worst bet ever.

These were the thoughts LeBron had as free agency
approached in July 2018. The answer ended up being
as simple as the announcement: LeBron was going
to L.A.

It may have been an imperfect basketball choice,
but it was a prudent and potentially brilliant business
choice. The older LeBron got, his business affairs had
only become more sophisticated and his future am-
bitions more grand. Carter once told me that LeBron
looked at his playing years as only a fraction of the time
he intended to make an impact on the world. He was
certainly not the first athlete to feel this way; many have
gone on to have massively successful post-playing lives
in business, philanthropy, politics, and sports. Namely

Magic Johnson, who was running the Lakers. LeBron wanted to leave all of these options open.

When looked at with some perspective, LeBron going to Miami in 2010 was a basketball decision, a way for LeBron to establish that he could be a champion. Going back to Cleveland in 2014 was a legacy decision, both to erase a black mark on his reputation and to secure his place in history by winning a championship in his hometown. The L.A. move in 2018 was a business decision, the culmination of fifteen years of learning, positioning, and exploiting the incredible fame and opportunities his basketball talents allowed. It was about how he was going to live for the next fifty years and what he'd leave his family when he was gone. That it came with nice weather, beaches, and an iconic basketball team was just the icing.

Less than three months after his move to L.A. was official, so, finally, was *Space Jam 2*. It had been under discussion for at least five years at that point. Different writers, directors, and producers had been attached at various points along the way. Carter and LeBron had seen and rejected numerous scripts. They had many meetings about it, discussions over dinners, brainstorming on private jets, and long talks after games when LeBron was in Cleveland and Carter was in L.A. on the front line. Once he was a Laker, though, the deal went through.

In the fall of 2018, SpringHill and Warner Bros.

made the announcement that *Space Jam 2* would go into production in the summer of 2019. They gathered a strong team with Ryan Coogler, who had scored a huge hit with his film *Black Panther* and would be a producer, and Terence Nance, who created a late-night sketch show for HBO called *Random Acts of Flyness* and would be the director. LeBron and Carter would produce and, of course, LeBron would star in the film alongside animated Warner Bros. characters from Looney Tunes, namely Bugs Bunny and Daffy Duck.

The first *Space Jam* film came out in 1996, but its roots were in a Super Bowl ad for Nike in 1992. It was the brainchild of the famous Portland firm Wieden+Kennedy, the same company that produced the pitch for LeBron when he came to Beaverton when he was a shoe free agent in 2003. Nike created the ad to pit Air Jordan against Hare Jordan, played by Bugs Bunny. It was one of the most memorable Super Bowl ads of that era, and Nike did another series of ads the following year.

Director Joe Pytka has said in interviews that Nike founder Phil Knight really was the reason *Space Jam* happened because he paid Warner Bros. for the rights to the characters, paid Jordan to shoot them in front of a green screen, and then bought the expensive Super Bowl commercial space that field-tested the idea. Then Knight didn't get any of the $230 million that the movie grossed in worldwide revenue, although

Jordan was wearing his signature shoes for everyone to see.

The real home run for the operation was in the merchandising. The *Chicago Tribune* reported there were seventy-eight tie-in products with Jordan's likeness that came out of *Space Jam* and that Warner Bros. realized $1.2 billion in sales with the Looney Tunes characters. The soundtrack that went with the film, which featured the single "I Believe I Can Fly" by R. Kelly, went platinum six times over. Money is still coming in from the film. That explains why Warner Bros. has so long been interested in getting LeBron to accept and embrace the role.

Jordan's take from the original film has never been reported. The dynamics of moviemaking in 2019 are much different than they were in the mid-1990s. But LeBron and Carter have been put in a position to profit significantly if all the parties can manufacture a hit. Seventeen producers were listed for the original film, including Jordan's agent, David Falk, and his longtime business manager, Curtis Polk. But Jordan was essentially an employee. Warner Bros. built him a gym to practice in when he wasn't filming, but he didn't have a house on the Warner Bros. lot like SpringHill does. He also didn't have a choice of two $20 million Brentwood mansions to sleep in.

*Space Jam 2* has a chance to make or break SpringHill and LeBron's future career in films. If it's a success,

Carter will probably be given a green light to go on and make other big-budget movies that could enhance the company. LeBron, if he's anywhere near as well regarded playing alongside the cartoons as he was alongside the actors in *Trainwreck*, would be able to perhaps expand his acting opportunities. When *Trainwreck* came out, LeBron was lauded for his performance and his ability to deliver funny lines. The *New Yorker* called it the "greatest movie performance by an active professional basketball player," which was high praise to be sure. Then again, he was playing himself, just as he'd played versions of himself in the other acting roles he'd been a part of. Maybe, just maybe, if LeBron comes off as the hero in *Space Jam 2* he could fulfill another dream that's been bouncing around his head over the years: to play a superhero.

It's all part of the evolution from teenage basketball star to young millionaire, pitchman, NBA star, businessman, NBA superstar, agent, documentary producer, Olympic champion, TV producer, business mogul, actor, entrepreneur, NBA champion, political activist, movie star, philanthropist, movie producer, franchisee, content creator, humanitarian, and, maybe someday superhero.

He has a show in which he and celebrity friends talk about everything from their childhood to politics in a barbershop. He has a documentary with former NBA player Al Harrington, who launched his own marijuana business. He was the voice of a yeti in the animated movie *Smallfoot*. And this only scratches the surface. Carter promises there's so much more in the pipeline and the incubator.

The journey has made LeBron internationally famous, hugely respected, and fabulously wealthy. If you believe him, though, he's still just getting started.

# EPILOGUE

So, is LeBron James a billionaire yet?

No, not yet. By the end of his current contract with the Los Angeles Lakers in 2022 he'll have earned about $391 million during nineteen NBA seasons, the most ever by an NBA player. Kevin Garnett holds the record, with $343 million. Kobe Bryant is right there, too, with $328 million. All before taxes, of course.

When combined with his equity in Liverpool FC, Blaze Pizza, Uninterrupted, SpringHill Entertainment, his real estate holdings, and his endorsement earnings, he may be getting close. In 2018, *Forbes* estimated LeBron had earned $765 million, including endorsements, in his career. He's known for being rather thrifty—some would call him downright cheap—so he likely still has a lot of it in various investment accounts.

"I'm not turning on data roaming. I'm not buying

no apps. I still got Pandora with commercials," LeBron said in an interview with Rachel Nichols on ESPN.

Former Cavs teammate Iman Shumpert said it annoyed him when they'd be listening to LeBron's phone while lifting weights and commercials would come on while he was streaming Pandora. LeBron didn't want to pay for the monthly fee to stream without ads. Then again, Shumpert said that if he had to put any teammate in charge of investing his money, it would be LeBron.

He's made a few bad investments. He said the worst was buying a house in Las Vegas at the height of the housing boom. But ever since his meeting with Warren Buffett, he's been safely invested with Berkshire Hathaway and blue chips. I once asked him how much Berkshire class A stock he owned—the shares reached more than $335,000 in value at one point in 2018—and he just smiled.

In 2014, Kevin Durant was the subject of a shoe bidding war between Under Armour and Nike. It was the hottest chase for a basketball player since LeBron in 2003, and it produced enormous numbers. Under Armour didn't have much of a shoe business at the time, and so it came forward and offered Durant a massive guaranteed deal. It couldn't rely on royalty sales that it hadn't ever been able to deliver at that point. Nike, who signed Durant to a $60 million deal when he turned pro in 2007, had full matching rights.

(As a side note, Adidas had offered Durant more, and he took less to sign with Nike.) Nike mulled but then matched, and Durant got a deal that reportedly could be worth up to $300 million over ten years. That took him past LeBron in the shoe game.

LeBron was in the middle of his second Nike deal when Durant's contract was finalized. He had a bigger business than Durant, and it opened the door for LeBron to renegotiate his contract. That's exactly what Maverick Carter did, and in 2016 LeBron signed a lifetime contract with Nike. Some sources have told me LeBron is regularly earning more than $30 million per year with Nike now, though the company hasn't confirmed any numbers.

Carter made some headlines when he gave an interview to *GQ* and indicated the Nike deal could be worth more than $1 billion by the end. That's conjecture; he's not guaranteed that much, and it's impossible to know how LeBron's signature shoes will sell after he's retired. Michael Jordan has a $1 billion annual business nearly twenty years since his retirement. But as any shoe company executive will tell you, there's only one Jordan. (OK, and one Chuck Taylor.)

"Jordan is an outlier. No one has ever sold shoes in retirement like Jordan," said Matt Powell, a sports apparel industry analyst. "It's hard to judge cycles. Over the last few years basketball shoes have gone out of fashion. LeBron's shoes have declined in sales since

2015. It could come back around. Going to L.A. could really help. We'll see."

Even if LeBron doesn't get to three commas with Nike, there are other ways. With the Liverpool investment as a basis, LeBron has his sights set on becoming a sports team owner. Carter has said that within ten years LeBron will own a sports team. It may seem rather ambitious, as every NBA team is now valued at over $1 billion, and who knows what that number will be a decade from now. Just looking at a big number and pondering how he'd be able to raise it, though, doesn't give Carter and LeBron enough credit. They've learned how to develop equity deals.

In 2017, Magic Johnson did an interview with Carter for the Uninterrupted platform that might as well have doubled as a course on wealth creation for superstar athletes. It didn't hurt that as team president of the Lakers at the time, Johnson was planning to try to sign LeBron a few months later. Johnson, of course, closed the deal after a meeting at LeBron's Brentwood house on his first night of free agency, July 1, 2018.

In the interview, Johnson told Carter that when he wanted to join an investment group for the purchase of the L.A. Dodgers in 2012, six different billionaires wanted to partner with him on a bid. It was going to be a competitive process, and having Johnson attached to a bid was quite valuable. Johnson interviewed the billionaires to choose who he wanted to align himself with, not the other way around. They had the money, but Johnson had something rarer—an impeccable reputation, respect in the sports world, and a Hall of Famer's credibility. In the end, Johnson partnered with Guggenheim Partners, and it was no surprise that the group got the team for $2 billion. Johnson became a minority partner, his net worth expanding along with his influence in pro sports.

When the Florida Marlins were for sale in 2017, a number of groups showed interest in buying. A group led by Derek Jeter ended up buying the team for $1.2 billion. Jeter became the CEO, running the team and even being criticized by fans and media when he ordered the front office to trade star Giancarlo Stanton to his former team, the Yankees. Jeter made these franchise-altering decisions even though his ownership stake was reported by the Associated Press to be just 4 percent. The majority of the money to buy the team came from a private equity magnate named Bruce Sherman, who became a billionaire by selling three companies to Buffett. (High finance is a small world.) Anyway, Jeter got control of a Major League Baseball team just three years after he retired, despite owning a relatively small percentage. Being a star athlete with a good name does have its perks. LeBron, of course, learned this lesson long ago.

"My gut tells me that down the line LeBron is going to own multiple sports teams around the world," said

Sam Kennedy, the Fenway Sports Group president. "And he'll be smart enough to hire smart people to run them and he'll sit back and monitor his global empire. He and Maverick have done really well financially and they know where they are going."

Getting money to buy a team may not be an issue for LeBron. The NBA will probably be eager for him to become an owner if a team becomes available and it can assist. In 2010, when the Charlotte Bobcats were up for sale, the league's board of governors bent its typical purchasing standards to ensure Jordan would buy a controlling interest in the team. Though Jordan took on a lot of debt from former owner Bob Johnson, the *Charlotte Observer* reported that Jordan's cash outlay to get his hands on the franchise was only $30 million.

A deal like that is probably impossible today, as franchise values have spiked and interest in teams has grown dramatically. Nonetheless, if a team was for sale and a retired LeBron indicated he was interested in leading an investment group, he probably would have no issue raising the cash or getting the NBA behind his bid. If Wachter is putting together the deal, you can count on LeBron being compensated with an appropriate percentage for his involvement.

All of this is to say that the story of LeBron's business is still very much unfolding. Whether he reaches his goal of team ownership or he finds a new pursuit is yet to be seen. His horizons are still expanding. For example, in late 2018 he launched a protein supplement business with Arnold Schwarzenegger—at long last he got into business with Wachter's biggest client. Maybe it becomes a giant; maybe it becomes nothing.

What we can see is this: LeBron's basketball career is drawing toward a close. He's got more games in his past than he does in his future. Over the years he's learned to shift his desire for victory off the floor. His pursuit of wins and his desire to employ strategy and maximize his advantages aren't going away. He loves the competition too much.

His passion to help disadvantaged children in his hometown has led to some of the most innovative actions in his life. He likes the way that feels. He doesn't want to stop doing that, either.

When LeBron was a teenager and reached a consciousness of his place in the world—that he'd been given a talent that placed him in a position to be one of the greatest ever at the sport he loved—he made a command decision to dedicate himself. He wanted to be in the best shape; he wanted to work tirelessly on his craft; he wanted to extend his career as long as possible. It was about maximizing the gift, to squeeze everything he could out of it.

His approach to business has taken the same route. He wants to take advantage of his fame; he wants to control and craft his image; he wants to leverage his position as long as he's in such endless demand. He wants to squeeze everything he can out of it, whether it's for his bank account, for his great-grandchildren's care, or for a kid who might be missing eighty-two days of fourth grade were it not for a promise he and LeBron made to each other.

When LeBron's story is over, it probably won't be about whether he made $1 billion or $5 billion. It will be what he wanted at age eighteen, at age thirty-four, at age eighty.

"I've been breaking the mold for a long time. That's what I want to do, I want to continue to break the mold for the next generation," LeBron said.

"I want it all."

# AFTERWORD TO THE TRADE EDITION

The Mercedes-Benz Arena resembles a giant white flying saucer that's landed on the banks of the Huangpu River, one of the architectural wonders of the Pudong district in Shanghai. It's been the site of NBA preseason games for years, as the NBA has made it an annual tradition to bring two teams to go on a brief, routine tour of China each October.

But in 2019, everything was far from routine. On Wednesday afternoon, October 9, LeBron and the Los Angeles Lakers were on the floor at the arena running through a practice attempting some semblance of normalcy. LeBron had played in China twice before on international NBA trips, once in 2007 with the Cleveland Cavs and again in 2012 with the Miami Heat in this very building. He had been to Shanghai many other times, having made more than fifteen trips to

China during his career, most of them as part of annual promotional trips for Nike. It had become a comfortable place for him. But not this day.

Before the Lakers were done, they were asked to leave the floor by arena officials. Behind them were workers who had come with equipment to sand the Vivo name off the hardwood floor. A year earlier the Chinese smartphone maker had paid millions to attach its name to the NBA's annual China Games, putting the branding right into the event's logo. Now the company wanted its name nowhere near the league and was scrambling to scrub its association by stripping signage from buildings, billboards, and buses immediately.

The root cause was a simple act from the previous week but one with massive implications. Daryl Morey, the general manager of the Houston Rockets, had posted a tweet supporting Hong Kong in its ideological and economic struggle with mainland China. This, in short, was a disaster for NBA business, becoming one of the biggest tests of LeBron's corporate acumen. It was a test many believe he failed.

For the previous five months there had been escalating protests in Hong Kong related to Chinese sovereignty. The protests had put many international corporations in a complicated position. For many Chinese, Hong Kong's status as part of the nation is intensely personal, and this makes any position on the matter a third-rail topic for companies that want to do business in China.

Morey's endorsement of the protests was quickly spread throughout China via social media and generated an intense reaction.

The timing was not ideal for the NBA. Less than two weeks earlier, the People's Republic of China had celebrated its seventieth anniversary. The centerpiece was a three-hour military parade in Beijing that led to both a high point in the country's patriotism as well as a new level of intensity to the protests. At the time, China and the United States were also engaged in a bubbling trade war, stoking further nationalistic views from the Chinese on any commentary from Americans.

Because of Yao Ming and his history with the Rockets, Houston was far and away the most popular team in China. Because of this, Morey was perhaps the most visible team GM, a visibility he cultivated by being active on social media, even on Chinese-based channels like the microblogging platform Weibo, where Morey maintained an account and put out messages in Mandarin.

Morey had posted the controversial message just as the Lakers and the Brooklyn Nets were in the air flying over the Pacific, coming for a week-long series of activities and two games, in Shanghai and Shenzhen.

All in all, it was a perfect storm. Any other basketball executive, it might've gone mostly unnoticed. A month earlier or later and there may not have been the same furor. And of the fifty-two weeks in the year, it just happened to be the one week the NBA teams were in the country. The result was a powder keg of backlash, ruining much of the business and goodwill plans the league had arranged and forcing both teams to largely hole up in their hotel.

I had been to China for three weeks in the summer of 2019 to cover the FIBA World Cup, and I had spent time in both Shanghai and Shenzhen. Before the games, members of Team USA had been briefed on the situation in Hong Kong and the Chinese feelings on the matter. They were strongly advised to stay clear of talking about it in the media or on social media. I had been advised to do so as well. The visa issued to me and other journalists covering the event didn't even allow me to return to mainland China if I left to visit Hong Kong while I was in Shenzhen, a short distance away.

While the Americans were in Shenzhen they played in a sports complex that had been partially converted into a staging area for military vehicles. Buses with riot gear positioned in the windows for maximum visibility lined the streets outside the arena where the World Cup was being held, which was less than a mile from the bridge to Hong Kong. The Americans—including coach Gregg Popovich, who is known for making his political opinions quite public—didn't say a word about the matter, and I had no intention of asking either. Before I left, I visited Beijing for the World Cup Finals and ran into preparations for the military parade. After midnight one evening, I had to walk a mile back to my hotel near Tiananmen Square because the military had closed blocks in every direction for a full practice. Soldiers manned the route eating their dinners—from KFC. In the morning, I was awakened by the roar of fighter jets. After opening my curtains, I saw a line of camouflaged vehicles moving down the street carrying what looked to be intercontinental ballistic missile launchers, with a formation of attack helicopters flying overhead, followed by heavy bombers. Part of being in China, I had learned, was to know the presence of the nation's power.

A month later, there was real frustration by the teams on the ground in Shanghai for the NBA games. LeBron was one of those fuming at Morey, who had sent the tweet while in Tokyo as part of a different NBA delegation that featured the Rockets. LeBron hadn't made his usual summer trip to China—he was filming *Space Jam 2* in L.A.—for Nike and instead had events planned all week to help promote his signature shoes.

China is a hugely important market for Nike. There are billions of feet, of course, but so many teenagers and young adults are into basketball that it's a vital growth market for the company. Just a few days before LeBron and the Lakers left for China, Nike reported quarterly results that showed nearly a 30 percent growth in footwear sales in China—versus a tepid 4 percent growth in the United States.

Chinese government officials were extremely upset with Morey's comments and the NBA's refusal to fire Morey or force him to resign. The games were removed from CCTV, the national television network, which also canceled all NBA games going forward. As did Tencent, a Chinese media conglomerate that streamed games to tens of millions of young fans, even though it had just agreed to a new five-year, $1.5 billion contract extension with the NBA. Just about every sponsor pulled its support as well. The Rockets lost tens of millions in previously arranged endorsement deals with Chinese companies. Anta, one of the largest shoe brands in Asia, suspended its association with the NBA.

Nike canceled several events as everyone was sobered by not only the potential loss of revenue but the civil unrest that could jeopardize the safety of the players on the ground. Further tension was caused when statements made by both Morey and the NBA failed to go far enough for the Chinese. It got to the point where NBA commissioner Adam Silver wasn't totally certain he'd be admitted into the country when he flew in for the games, if the games even took place.

When Silver met with the teams inside a Ritz-Carlton hotel a few miles from the arena, LeBron spoke for the players in the room and made the point that players shouldn't have to address the media given their tenuous position. There was almost no way to do so without causing more backlash, be it in China and its clearly defined position or back home where Morey was being cheered by some as an advocate for freedom of speech.

Silver and the players had an emotional meeting, but the commissioner ultimately agreed with LeBron that the players should not speak to the media while in China. They did play the two games, under significant tension, with many in the crowds at the two games waving Chinese flags.

When LeBron got back to the United States, however, he did speak. And his problems only magnified. After more than a week of silence while he was in China, James had consulted with his inner circle about how to delicately address the situation.

There were two competing factors in his thinking. One was his long-term relationship with China, which was fragile and in which every word had to be considered. The other was a fuming anger at Morey. There was already some baggage there, as Morey had released Carmelo Anthony without warning the year before, putting his career in jeopardy. Then over the summer, Morey had traded Chris Paul to the Oklahoma City Thunder within days of assuring Paul he wouldn't be dealt. These are two of LeBron's best friends, and he felt Morey hadn't treated either with respect.

Now Morey had done something LeBron felt hadn't just put him in harm's way financially but created an uncomfortable situation for him and his peers while they were in China. That Morey faced no punishment from the league—Silver had supported his right to free speech—had only further infuriated James. What would've happened, LeBron openly wondered to friends, if it were a player who had taken a sledgehammer to the league's billion-dollar business partner?

With this on his mind, LeBron spoke in front of dozens of cameras before a Lakers preseason game:

> Yes, we all do have freedom of speech. But at times, there are ramifications for the negative that can happen when you're not thinking about others and you're only thinking about yourself. I don't want to get into a feud with Daryl Morey, but I believe he wasn't educated on the situation at hand and he spoke. So many people could have been harmed—not only financially, but physically, emotionally, spiritually. So just be careful about what we tweet, what we say and what we do. Yes, we do have freedom of speech, but there can be a lot of negative that comes with that, too.

A Lakers spokeswoman quickly ended the interview, but it was too late. LeBron's words came off to many as being both pro-China and anti-free speech, red meat for politicians who circled with fresh attacks. LeBron's spite was meant to be aimed at Morey, but he hadn't been precise in his language—an unusual mistake for him—and he would pay for it.

Within ninety minutes, the reaction was so negative that LeBron and the Lakers felt he had to follow up with some sort of additional statement. He wasn't playing in the game that night, and as his teammates readied for the tip-off, he crafted a new comment that he posted to Twitter just minutes before coming out to the bench to watch the game:

> Let me clear up the confusion. I do not believe there was any consideration for the consequences and ramifications of the tweet. I'm not discussing the substance. Others can talk about that. My team and this league just went through a difficult week. I think people need to understand what a tweet or statement can do to others. And I believe nobody stopped and considered what would happen. Could have waited a week to send it.

He was pointing out nuances, but the topic was just too volatile. For the first time since *The Decision* nine years earlier, LeBron had made a real faux pas in the court of public opinion. He was battered in op-eds, on talking head political shows, and on social media for taking a position that seemed anti-American and was certainly anti-Hong Kong.

"Every word that I say is going to be broken down to how you feel I said it. It comes with the territory. It's a small bump in the road but time heals all," he said the next day, trying to manage what had become significant fallout. "I'm not perfect, obviously, I just try to do things that make my family proud and make my fans proud. It's a tough situation we're all in. . . . It was a challenging trip for all of us in China, and if you were not there, you just can't relate."

Just how extensive the damage wasn't immediately clear. After decades of building fan support in China and LeBron riding that wave with Nike and other businesses, everything took a step backward. The furor over LeBron's comments died quickly in Los Angeles and the rest of the American media, though opponents in the future will likely come back to them. Especially conservative politicians, who can weaponize them if LeBron campaigns for Democrats as he has in the past. The bigger issue was access and approval in the Chinese marketplace.

In addition to the shoes there's also *Space Jam 2*. The Chinese government is selective about which foreign movies it allows to be released in the country. During the mid-2010s there was an agreement with Hollywood that thirty-four movies per year would get into the largest-growing movie market in the world, nearing $9 billion in ticket sales in 2018. But that agreement has ended, and the government now controls the number as it sees fit. That has made getting movies into China a sometimes political game, with potentially hundreds of millions at stake per film.

For LeBron, SpringHill Productions, and Warner Bros., getting *Space Jam 2* into China when it's released in 2021 is vital. And if it gets in, then he has to be concerned about Chinese fans wanting to see it. The original *Space Jam*, released in 1996, made more than $140 million in international box office sales, when the basketball craze in China was still in its infancy. This was a major reason why LeBron should have been careful when handling this unexpected political firestorm.

The incident was a reminder that LeBron has entered the deep end of the pool when it comes to off-court business. In late 2018, on his HBO show *The Shop*, LeBron took aim at NFL owners when he said: "In the NFL they got a bunch of old white men owning teams and they got a slave mentality." He had his reasons for saying it, but in doing so he potentially alienated a group of influential power brokers with whom he may want to do business some day. Some of the NFL owners also own NBA teams, and that's a group he may want to join in the future.

In responding to the situation in China, he found himself in another messaging and branding pothole. There are probably more to come in the future. For the most part, James has navigated this road successfully.

But the higher the stakes, the shadier the path can become.

"I'm not a politician, it's a huge political thing; but I am a leader," LeBron said, reflecting on the situation once things had calmed down. "If you don't think you should speak one thing then maybe you shouldn't have to."

That, in the end, may have been the lesson LeBron took away from the ordeal. It's the sort of thing he might have to apply as he continues his chase for his first billion dollars. And then, he expects, his second. And it's another reminder that even though his basketball days are perhaps nearing the stretch run, there is a lot of the LeBron story left to unfold.

Stay tuned.

# ACKNOWLEDGMENTS

LeBron James is one of the most watched, written about, and talked about athletes in history. His story is always evolving, in part because he has embraced change throughout his career. That has provided me with a tremendous opportunity to chronicle his journey. It is a fortunate position to be in, something I will never take for granted.

LeBron and his closest friends and associates have been with him for twenty years. This means there was a time when they were naïve newcomers to the basketball and business world. When they arrived in the NBA, I arrived as a naïve newcomer too. Over the last two decades it's been fascinating to watch them grow, overcoming failure and finding successes. Though my path has been different, it's often run parallel. We have often watched and critiqued each other's work. There have been times when we wondered just what the hell the other was doing. There have been times of genuine closeness and times of genuine distance. It's been a challenging, enriching, and fulfilling voyage.

So first I will give thanks to LeBron James, Maverick Carter, and Rich Paul for their access and insight for the past twenty years. I also want to thank Adam Mendelsohn, who was a resource throughout the project.

Thank you to Aaron Goodwin, Steve Stoute, Kristopher Belman, Matt Powell, Sam Kennedy, Jim Gray, John Skipper, Luke Wood, Darren Rovell, Rick Anguilla, Ellen Lucey, Brian Berger, Nick DePaula, Rachel Nichols, Jason Lloyd, Dave McMenamin, Joe Vardon, Jon Wile, Tim Bontemps, and numerous other sources who were willing to give their time and share their experiences for this book.

A special note of appreciation to Kevin Arnovitz, whose ingenuity and creativity as an editor, colleague, and friend helped make this and many other pieces over the years possible.

Without the backing of Rob King, Lauren Reynolds, Cristina Daglas, and Chris Ramsay at ESPN, this project wouldn't have been completed.

I'm grateful for the support of Sean Desmond and his team at Hachette Book Group and Daniel Greenberg and his team at LGR Literary Agency.

Finally, none of this has been possible without the patience and support of my family, particularly my wife, Maureen Fulton.

# INDEX

Lawson, Ty, 81
LeBron James Family Foundation
  adding GED program, 207
  donating to National Museum of
    African American History
    and Culture, 209
  grant releases, 204
  I Promise program, 202–204
  King for Kids Bikeathon, 193–194
  launch of, 194–195
  launching I Promise School, 207
    –209
  Merritt as board member of, 209
  Michele Campbell in charge of,
    201–202
  office move to Akron, 201
  operating in the red, 195
  sponsors for, 204
  University of Akron partnership,
    205–206
  Wheels for Education, 202
LeBron James Skills Academy, 79–
  82
LeBron Summit, 102–103
The LeBrons (cartoon series), 169–
  170
LeBron's Dream Team (paperback),
  134
Lee, Spike, 19
Leibovitz, Annie, 104
Lennon, John, 121
Levine, Jay, 189
Levy, David, 189
Lionsgate, 132
Liverpool Football Club, 171, 174, 190
Lopez, Brook and Robin, 81
Los Angeles Lakers, 212–213, 225
Love, Kevin, 216
LRMR Marketing. See also Carter,
  Maverick; Mims, Randy; Paul,
  Rich
  creating LeBron Summit, 102–
    103
  Cub Cadet and, 85
  establishing legitimacy in finan-
    cial world, 138

  as failed athlete marketing com-
    pany, 90–91
  founding of, 77–78
  hiring Buzz Bissinger, 100
  hiring research firm, 100–101
  leveraging relationships with
    college coaches, 82–83
  Microsoft and, 85–86
  multistage plan, 82
  negotiating second deal with
    Nike, 138
  profiled in Advertising Age, 103
  Rich Paul leaving, 139
Lucas, John, 40
Lucey, Ellen, 155

Magic Johnson, 74
Main Street Advisors, 113
Manziel, Johnny, 90
marketing strategy
  gifting of other influencers, 125
  trading ownership for marketing
    rights, 171–173
Marquis Jet, 109–110
Marsh, Joe, 17–20, 94
Martin, Trayvon, 198–199
Mason, Harvey, Jr., 99
Matthews, Wesley, 81
McDonald's, 136, 175–176
McDonald's All-American Game, 62
McGee, Willie, 25
McGrady, Tracy, 27
Mendelsohn, Adam, 179–180, 183–
  184, 189
Merritt, Lynn
  allowing Carter to grow, 73
  at Cavs games, 69
  LeBron and, 47–48, 183
  on LeBron James Family Foun-
    dation's board, 209–210
  offering Carter internship at
    Nike, 35
  recruiting/advancing stars, 31–32
  at UCLA showcase event, 26
Miami Heat, 163–165, 197, 199, 204,
  216

# ABOUT THE AUTHOR

**Brian Windhorst** has covered the NBA for ESPN since 2010. He was the daily beat writer on the Cleveland Cavaliers for the *Akron Beacon Journal* and *Cleveland Plain Dealer* from 2003 to 2010, and he began covering LeBron James in 1999. He is also the co-author of three books, including the *New York Times* bestseller *Return of the King, The Franchise,* and *The Making of an MVP.*